W9-BHY-236

VOICES FROM THE NATIONS

We the Vietnamese

VOICES FROM THE NATIONS

WE THE CHINESE: *Voices from China* edited by Deirdre and Neale Hunter

WE THE RUSSIANS: *Voices from Russia* edited by Colette Shulman

WE THE BURMESE: *Voices from Burma* edited by Helen G. Trager

WE THE VIETNAMESE

Voices from Vietnam

Edited by François Sully

with the Assistance of Marjorie Weiner Normand

Preface by Donald Kirk

PRAEGER PUBLISHERS
New York • Washington • London

"In Search of the Enemy of Man" is reprinted from *Vietnam: Lotus in a Sea of Fire* by Thich Nhat Hanh. Copyright © 1967 by Hill and Wang, Inc. Reprinted by permission of Hill and Wang, Inc.

"East Meets West in the PX" by Raymond A. Sokolov © *Newsweek*, Inc., July 29, 1968. Reprinted by permission.

"The Vietcong's 10-Point Proposal in Paris" © 1969 by The New York Times Company. Reprinted by permission.

"How Vietnam Contained China" and "Why Every American Should Read *Kim Van Kieu*" by Tran Van Dinh are reprinted from *Washingtonian Magazine* with the permission of the author.

"Flower of Tears" by Ha Huyen Chi, translated by Do Lenh Thuon, *Tien Phong* (Vanguard), 1966. Reprinted by permission of the publisher.

"Don't Pick the Flower When It Is Blooming" and "The Mother of 'Gio Linh.'" Reprinted by permission of the author.

PRAEGER PUBLISHERS
111 Fourth Avenue, New York, N.Y. 10003, U.S.A.
5, Cromwell Place, London S.W.7, England

Published in the United States of America in 1971
by Praeger Publishers, Inc.

Library of Congress Catalog Card Number: 75–95693

Printed in the United States of America

CONTENTS

PART THREE. A *Poetic People: Literature and Art*

LIST OF ILLUSTRATIONS

PREFACE

By Donald Kirk

"A taste for adventure . . . courage before danger"—so Gerard Sully described his brother François after the latter's death in a helicopter crash in South Vietnam on February 23, 1971. There was far more to François Sully: He was a man to whom a pleasant conversation, a skillfully executed object of art, a bottle of vintage wine were equally important. And beneath this level lay a deep sensitivity to the people of Vietnam.

In his twenty-four years as a war correspondent in Indochina, Sully always perceived the small details, the nuances that mean more, in the final analysis, than military charts and rows of statistics. "The wounded are carried in one direction . . ." he cabled *Newsweek* four years, almost to the day, before his death. "The dead go another way. I walk to the mess hall for a meal of leftover beef. An old French war song comes back to me—'*Chacun son tour . . . Aujourd'hui le tien, demain le mien*'—To each his turn . . . Today yours, tomorrow mine."

With this poignant memory, Sully caught the humdrum terror of the war, which has dragged on so long. As a Frenchman who had joined the resistance against Germany in World War II, Sully empathized with the struggle of the Vietnamese for some semblance of integrity—and relief. His awareness was based not on ideological leanings but on a feeling for individuals.

Much of Vietnamese life revolves around its young people, especially students and soldiers. Sully's rapport with the young, both on the campus and in the field, gave him special insights into their basic attitudes toward the war. Many are not at all interested in conspiring with the Viet Cong. They share much the same disillusionment as young people in America and want an end to the seemingly endless destruction and slaughter. While agents of the National Liberation Front have doubtless exploited such sentiments, the desire to return to peacetime values has underlain student demonstrations for nearly a decade. In the universities and high schools, student organizations, some of them clandestine, campaign against political leaders who represent a system that seems alien to them. Many other young Vietnamese simply prefer to pursue their self-interest. Thousands have deserted from the army, for instance, to rejoin their families or to till the land. Still more have performed their military duties only to avoid the risk of arrest or reprisal. The streets of Saigon and other large towns are crowded with young men who have managed, somehow, to avoid the draft. Numbers of them have turned to petty crime, but others work quietly as clerks, mechanics, laborers—generally leaving demonstrations to their more articulate peers in the universities. And still others have fought willingly and heroically.

The quality of life here, as anywhere, reveals itself in everyday happenings as well as in the headlines. Sully caught this quality in his choice of materials for this volume. The tragedy of Sully's death was that it prevented him from putting his own thoughts on Vietnamese life into a novel or other book. Have Americans, in their concern with the war, had time to think about the loves and fears of young Vietnamese? About the centuries of literary, artistic, and military traditions that inevitably influence their attitudes? Through the almost forgotten literature of the Vietnamese themselves, Sully attempted to reveal some of these feelings and traditions.

His death prevented him from obtaining formal permission to reprint some of these articles. Praeger Publishers asked me to see what I could do. Some of the writers and editors are in North Vietnam, others defied my attempts to locate them, but I am sure they would be only too glad to see their writings disseminated in America. Nguyen Lau, for instance, the editor of the former *Saigon Daily News,* whom I knew personally, was arrested and jailed. If I am still here when this book is published, I will try to send him a copy in prison.

This anthology, then, serves not only as a memorial to Sully's career as an Indochinese correspondent—but also as an indication of the book he himself might have written. Perhaps, in addition, it will encourage some of its readers to view Vietnam more as an array of deeply individual human conflicts than as a military or ideological "confrontation" delineated by propaganda.

Majestic Hotel, Saigon
April, 1971

The editors of Praeger Publishers wish to extend their sincerest thanks to the anonymous or insufficiently credited contributors to this book.

INTRODUCTION

By François Sully and Marjorie Weiner Normand

This is a book about Vietnam, North and South. It is about a country torn by war and revolution for more than twenty-five years. In fact, Vietnam is at present two countries, or, at the least, two completely separate political entities, divided by a partition line imposed at a foreign conference in 1954. Each of these two bitterly and violently competing parts of one land has a government, an army, a territorial base—and each one claims to represent the true and legitimate interests of all the Vietnamese. The Vietnamese themselves, for the most part, refuse to accept the partition of their land as permanent. Yet they have been unable to resolve the differences between the opponents or to decisively opt for one or the other. Part of the problem lies in the fact that each of the two Vietnamese governments has made an alliance with one of the two world "superblocs"; this has drawn the Vietnamese conflict into the international arena, where the voices of the Vietnamese are often subordinated to international political considerations.

The important experiences of the Vietnamese in this century have been cataclysmic: colonialism, nationalism, revolution, war against the French, war against the Americans, and war against each other. All of this has impinged drastically on the daily life of Vietnamese in North and South, urban and rural. Hardly an inch of Vietnamese territory has escaped

Saigon's central market was built by the French about fifty years ago. The billboards advertise a local toothpaste.

bombing and war devastation: all facets of life in Vietnam must be viewed in the context of war.

This book attempts a nonpartisan portrait of Vietnamese life, without bias and without omitting any representative group that, by its influence or role, contributes to making Vietnam what it is today: a singularly fascinating country, complex, diverse, exasperating, bewildering, yet enticing. We examine not only North and South Vietnam, with their separate and vastly different administrative structures and sociopolitical systems, but also another Vietnam, the underground realm of the National Liberation Front (NLF). An active revolutionary movement in South Vietnam, the NLF has had a distinctive influence on Southern life and has created a subculture of its own, including its own artists, writers, politicians, and folklore.

Finding a way to define the Vietnamese is hard indeed, and any definition is inevitably couched in generalities. It has been said that the Vietnamese is suspicious of others, especially foreigners, and tends to feel comfortable only in his large family circle. In spite of this, the Vietnamese is gregarious; he hates physical loneliness. Traditional rural society was centered in the village, and the village constituted the peasant's whole world. Because communication between the isolated and self-sufficient villages was difficult, regional differences, rooted in history, became quite pronounced.

North Vietnam, the "cradle" of Vietnamese civilization, has produced a type reputed to be overly ambitious, sometimes quarrelsome, and aggressive in all his pursuits. The Northerner supposedly is convinced of his intellectual superiority and is contemptuous of those from other regions, especially the easygoing Southerners. North Vietnam has also given birth to many of Vietnam's most famous revolutionaries, and the Northerner's reputation for the ruthless and single-minded pursuit of a cause, an ideal, or an interest has led to fears of a Northern "takeover," especially in the South.

The man from central Vietnam is more attached to preserving the Confucian traditions of his land and the cultural heritage of his ancestors. It was in the center, in the lovely city of Hue, that the imperial court held sway, and there the emperors' tombs are still revered. The center is a proud land, where even peasant women wear their Sunday-best *ao dai* (the Vietnamese women's national dress) to buy a brace of ducks at the market. No one knows what the men think. But it is known that they like political power and prestige, that they respect intellectual pursuits but make poor businessmen. Life is hard in central Vietnam, and austere, and Western ways are slow to take hold.

The Southerner is a product of his environment: South Vietnam was long a frontier region, settled by Vietnamese pioneers in a "march South" that continued through the nineteenth century. Land in the South is fertile, and in peacetime life has tended to be slower and easier than elsewhere in Vietnam. The Southerner has a reputation—perhaps because French economic and cultural influence has been more dominant in the South than in the other regions—of being more open to Western ideas, more adaptable to progress, less rigid and inhibited by traditional ways of doing things. Today he plows his rice paddies behind a pair of water buffaloes. Tomorrow he will drive a shiny new farm tractor. To acquire upper-middle-class respectability is his great ambition, and his brother Vietnamese tend to consider him "bourgeois" and materialistic.

These descriptions, vague and imprecise, do not begin to encompass all the Vietnamese character, for considerations other than those of geographical location have come to play a dominant role in shaping the lives of Vietnamese today. The war, and the social and economic upheavals accompanying it, have created new classes that do not fit into traditional Vietnamese society. In old Vietnam, the mandarins and scholars were the most respected class, and the peasants ranked next; merchants and soldiers were low on the social scale. French colonial policy broke down traditional class structure, and the long, arduous wars of the past thirty years completed the destruction of rural society. Now, enormous power is wielded by military mandarins: inbred, secretive, many trained abroad, and all fully conscious of their importance. A new and growing class of Vietnamese petty bourgeois appeared under French rule. Using their money as a cushion against the rigors of war, they try to lead a quiet existence with their television sets, their cars, and their retreats in the cool hills of Dalat or on the Ving Tau beaches. However, it has become increasingly difficult to ignore the existence of the war, even in the urban centers, for the fighting has caused a mass exodus to the cities. The swollen population centers are urbanized but not industrialized and do not provide enough jobs for the impoverished refugees, now a kind of rootless proletariat. Then there are the revolutionaries, men willing to endure hardship and deprivation in pursuit of their ideals. Finally, in North Vietnam especially, there is a "new breed" of men, willing to use the apparatus of government to reshape the social and political structure of society and to substitute "socialist construction" for more traditional goals.

To understand the roots of the Vietnamese conflict and to become acquainted with the Vietnamese themselves, one must delve into events not only of this century but of the more remote past, for Vietnam has a long and proud history. One will learn who the Trung sisters were; discover what happened at the Dien Hong conference and why the armies of Genghis Khan finally had to retreat from Vietnam; read how Emperor Gia Long reunited Vietnam but why the eventual price to pay was French occupation. One can then move on to documents dealing with more recent aspects of Vietnamese history, much of which, at least to the Vietnamese, sounds like a repetition of the past. Even a look at Vietnamese literature and art is helpful. Reading extracts from the national epic, *Kim Van Kieu*—a marvelous story of impossible love and filial devotion that all Vietnamese can recite by heart—will help the reader to understand some Vietnamese ideals and virtues that, within a modern context, are still part of the Vietnamese soul.

Finally, one can come face to face with his own knowledge of Vietnam, as enlightened by television, newspapers, and the awful fact that Americans and Vietnamese are dying there every day. Perhaps this book can help to explain in part how the Vietnamese themselves became embroiled in the war and why the United States intervened—and who, indeed, the Vietnamese are.

PART ONE

Land and People: Beliefs and Customs

NATURAL RESOURCES

"GLIMPSES OF VIETNAM," BY *Tran Xuan Ly*

The shape of Vietnam has often been likened to a bamboo pole balancing a basket of rice at each end. The rice baskets represent the rich alluvial deltas of the Red River in the North and the Mekong River in the South; the pole is the narrow mountain range connecting them. This peculiar geographical configuration has, in effect, created two great areas of population. The lack of easy communication links between them has had a profound political influence on the Vietnamese nation, torn between two centers of attraction. With North Vietnam, the country has a foothold on the mainland of Asia, a poor region imbued with China's overpowering cultural heritage. The southern peninsula, only recently settled by ethnic Vietnamese, is part of the South Seas region, a tropical melting pot of races and cultures, a varied mixture of cults and religions influenced by its closer maritime relations with the Western world. Perhaps the best thumbnail description of Vietnam is that of a Vietnamese intellectual, who likens his country to a surrealist painting "with many bits of different shapes and color in it."

Between the great ports of Hong Kong and Singapore, slightly out the way of the main sea lanes crisscrossing the South China Sea, Vietnam—North and South—flanks the eastern coast of the Southeast Asian peninsula. This balcony on the Pacific, as earlier European explorers used to call it, is part of the underbelly of the Asian continent. Long and narrow, it curves down in a rough S-shape for 1,100 miles from China in the north, pinches at the center to less than fifty miles, and broadens southwestward into the Gulf of Siam. Vietnam shares its western border with Laos and Cambodia and with these two nations was known as French Indochina for more than half a century before World War II.

The Truong Son mountain chain stretches nearly the length of Vietnam, linking the country's two large delta regions—those of the Red River in the far north and of the Mekong River in the extreme south. Land area totals 127,000 square miles (330,000 square kilometers), about the size of the State of New Mexico.

In this tropical and predominantly agricultural country, an estimated 80 per cent of the 38 million people are farmers. They are concentrated in the deltas of the Red and Mekong rivers and in scattered villages and hamlets of the lowland coastal areas. Rice is their major food crop. Rubber is an important export product in the lightly industrialized, mineral-deficient South. The less fertile North has coal and ores for its nascent industrial base. Fishing is of great importance.

A short, handsome, fine-boned people, at least 85 per cent of the population are ethnically Vietnamese, or Annamese, as they were called in earlier centuries. The largest minority group is Chinese, perhaps numbering one million, mostly in the South. There are some three million aboriginal peoples, collectively called Montagnards (mountaineers) by the French, who live in the semi-isolation of the highlands. In the lowlands live several hundred thousand people of the same stock as the majority of people in neighboring Cambodia.

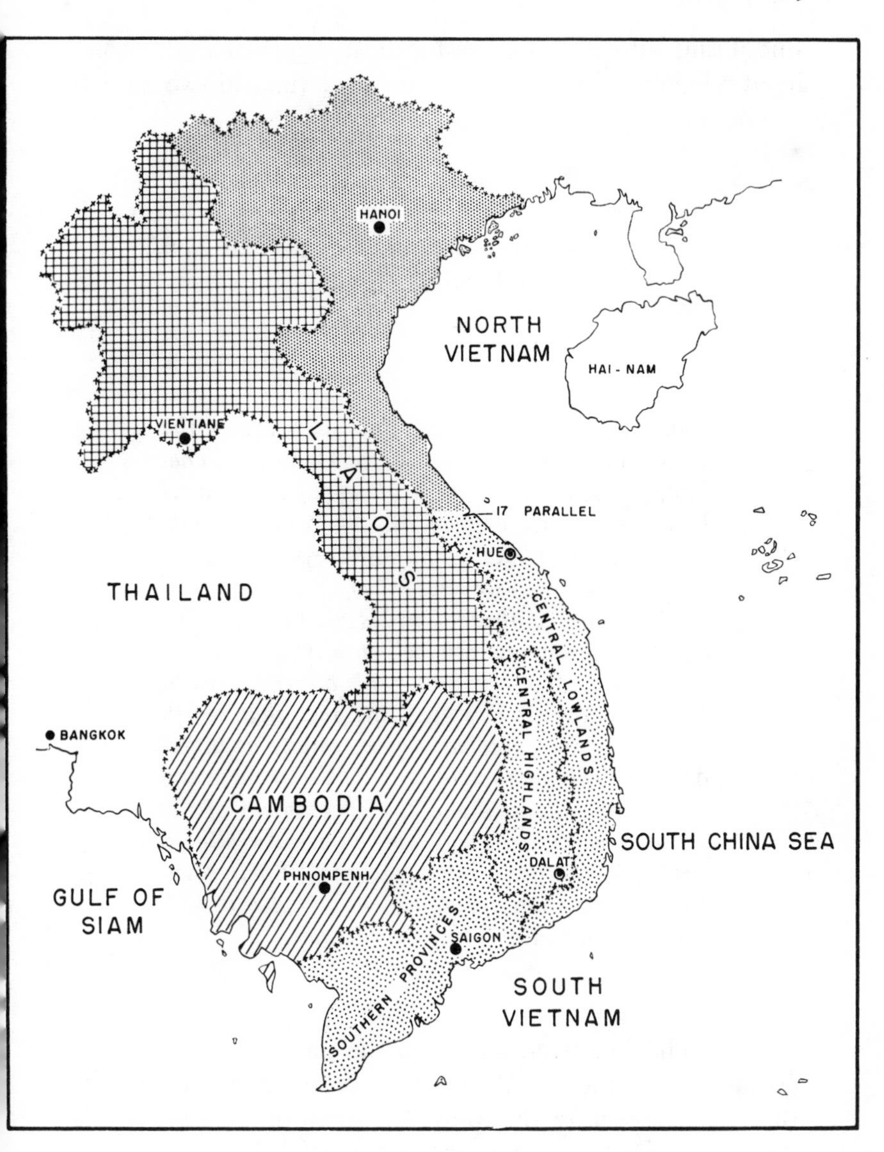

Map of Vietnam

Buddhism, infused with Confucianist precepts, is the dominant religious faith of the country. An estimated two million people are Roman Catholics.

"IN THE HEART OF OUR COUNTRY," BY *Thai Lan* (in *Hanoi Tien Phong*)

This article was published some years ago in the Hanoi Tien Phong (The Call of Hanoi) *by Thai Lan, a young technician working for the Central Directorate of Geology of the Democratic Republic of Vietnam (DRV). The author speaks in glowing terms of the treasures of minerals, ores, and other products embedded in his country's soil. Because of the war and the lack of development capital, only a minor fraction of this potential wealth has been mined. However, the fact that North Vietnam's soil contains a great variety of useful ores has been long established by Vietnamese and European geologists, and the government of the DRV is eager to exploit this mineral wealth to further its industrialization programs. South Vietnam, on the contrary, appears to be richer in agricultural land than in useful minerals.*

"The forests are gold and the sea is silver." This old proverb praises the abundant natural resources of our country. But when repeating this proverb, many of us immediately think that our forests are a repository of ivory and valuable timber, while our waters are rich only in priceless marine products.

If this were all, then our wealth would not amount to much. To understand fully the meaning of this proverb, we must alter it: "In the heart of our land are endless treasures."

Indeed, in the past five years, geological research units have been prospecting and examining our soil. They have helped dig some 100,000 cubic meters of ditches, wells, pits, and so forth, through hills and mountains. They have bored 300 to 400 meters deep into the heart of the earth to explore for mineral ores for our industry.

In their recapitulative report at the end of 1960, these geological research units enthusiastically announced that more than 3,000 mineral-ore locations have been discovered in North Vietnam.

Two beds of coal extend from Ke Bao island to Thai Nguyen, and from Hoa Binh to Ninh Binh—a total length (for the two beds) of some 360 kilometers. Coal mines have also been found in Lang Son, Cao Bang, Tuyen Quang, Yen Bai, Thanh Hoa, and Nghe An provinces. In addition to brown and soft coals, hard coal—the chief material in making coke, which is used in the metallurgical industry—has been found.

In addition to coal, our soil also contains beds of iron. Iron mines can be found in various places in the Tay Bac and Viet Bac zones, in the northern part of central Vietnam, and along the northern coastline. The two most important iron mines are the Thai Nguyen and Red River mines. In Thai Nguyen, we are setting up our first cast-iron and steel industrial zone.

Recently, in Cao Bang and Ha Giang provinces, we uncovered bauxite ore of excellent quality, which is suitable for the refining of aluminum and the manufacture of fireproof bricks. At present, we can say that our country is one of the richest nations in bauxite in the world.

In addition, our soil contains a large chromite bed equal to one-tenth the chromite ore possessed by other nations. Workers at the Co-Dinh enterprise are presently striving hard to exploit and refine chromite ore.

We have discovered 150 locales where lead and zinc are present. Most of these locales are situated in Bac Can, Tuyen Quang, and Thai Nguyen provinces. The Cho Dien and Tu Le mining zones are particularly rich in these ores. In one of the two zones we also have discovered a silver bed. These two zones will provide abundant raw materials for the Quang Yen zinc-refining enterprise, which is to resume and develop its activities further.

In addition to the metals already mentioned, our soil contains tin, wolfram, gold, copper, manganese, and so forth. We have also discovered titanium, which is used in refining a special steel necessary for the aeronautic industry. Radioactive ores have also been found, and our geologists hope to discover petroleum in the Red River Delta.

In the heart of our soil, there are immense resources of such nonferrous materials as mica and feldspar. At present, we are exploiting the kaolin, or porcelain clay, and supplying it to the Hai Duong porcelain factory and to all pottery workshops throughout North Vietnam. We are also exploiting limestone and supplying it to the Haiphong cement factory.

The most valuable resource of all is the Lao Cai apatite mine—one of the largest in the world. This apatite mine lies along the right bank of the Red River, running from the Bo stream to Bat Xat—a distance of 40 kilometers. Even were we to exploit this mine with modern equipment, it would not be exhausted for another century.

The Lao Cai mine has supplied apatite for export to the People's Republic of China, Poland, Rumania, and Japan in recent years, in addition to providing apatite for the Van Dien factory, which yearly produces approximately 10,000 tons of phosphorous fertilizer. In coming years, when the Phu Tho superphosphate plant is completed, the Lao Cai mine will provide, from its unlimited resources, apatite for manufacturing the phosphorous fertilizer necessary for our agriculture.

Our soil is rich in natural resources. To serve the five-year plan [1960–65] or another longer plan, our geologic units—with help from brother countries—are employing geophysical methods involving electricity, magnetic fields, and radioactivity to carry out superficial research. Recently, they have even used aircraft to carry out aerial exploration. With today's modern equipment, we are fully capable of discovering many other new ore beds in the near future. Whenever an ore site has been carefully explored, an enterprise to carry out processing will be set up, thus showing that our geologists have been there.

RURAL LIFE

"VIETNAMESE COUNTRY LIFE," BY *Nguyen Dinh Hoa* (in *Vietnam Inquirer*, June, 1968)

Dr. Nguyen Dinh Hoa, former Director of Cultural Affairs, Education Ministry of Vietnam, is at present serving at the Vietnamese Embassy in Washington. He is also the author of many books on the Vietnamese language. His article on Vietnamese rural life, reproduced below, describes the rhythm of life in an idyllic past time and can help the reader understand Vietnamese nostalgia for the past. However, this tranquil, well-ordered life bears little resemblance to the present turbulent, dangerous existence of the Vietnamese farmer in the midst of war. In fact, the absence of any mention of the generally hard lot of the Vietnamese farmer even before the war—the struggle for survival against natural calamities, the pressures of avaricious landlords, high usury rates, land taxes, and so on—leads one to the conclusion that this was an idealized form of village life even in the past.

Traditionally, Vietnamese society is said to consist of four strata of people (*tu dan*), listed in order of importance as follows: the mandarins and scholars (*si*); the farmers (*nong*); the craftsmen (*cong*); and the merchants (*thuong*). Each claims that its members contribute a vital share to Vietnamese society. A popular saying, however, seems to show that this order of ranking is not always true in real life: "Scholar ranks first, then comes the peasant. But when rice runs out, and you run wildly about, the peasant comes first, and scholar second." The truth of this saying becomes obvious when one realizes that Vietnam is a country with an agricultural economy and that the farming population constitutes roughly 90 per cent of the total.

A Simple Diet

Despite his pre-eminent role, the Vietnamese farmer leads a simple life. His diet consists of the staple food, rice, to which are added corn, sweet potatoes, taro, manioc yams, arrowroot, soybeans, eggs, and whatever fish is available in the immediate vicinity. Only on special occasions—the birth of a child, the wedding of a daughter, or the death of a parent—does the Vietnamese peasant kill a chicken, a duck, or a pig. Although for such good reasons wealthy families may entertain lavishly for days, and many a fatted pig, cow, and water buffalo may be doomed to death, the farmer's daily meals are composed mostly of salted vegetables and salted fish. Meat, when it does appear, is considered a great treat for both the guest and the host.

Besides tea, the national drink, some people take rice wine with their meals. Food is nearly always served on a round or rectangular tray made of wood or copper. Members of the family sit cross-legged around the tray, which is placed in the center of a low bed. Each person uses a porcelain bowl and chopsticks. These are made of bamboo or wood, although well-to-do households are proud to display ebony or lacquer ones. Men, women, and children partake of the meal at the

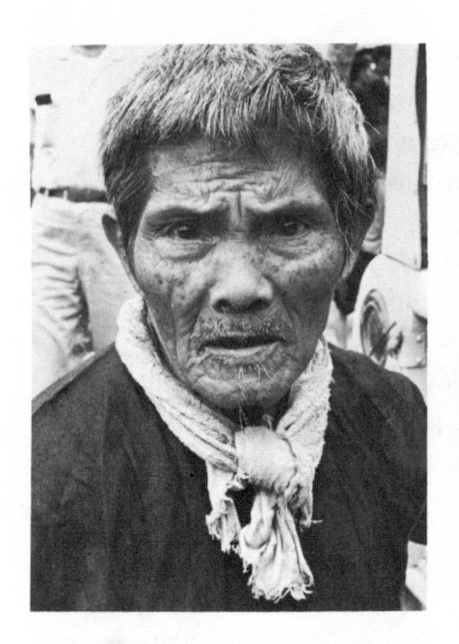

A farmer at day's end; another farmer and his water buffalo prepare a flooded rice field for transplanting.

same time, the mother or her daughter-in-law sitting nearest to the rice pot so as to be able to serve the others. Meat and vegetables, very often just boiled, are dipped in a fish sauce called nuoc mam. Very often after a meal the women chew a quid of betel, and the men smoke a bamboo water pipe and drink many cups of tea. Innumerable varieties of rice cakes—using glutinous rice, soybeans, and cane sugar as ingredients—and rice gruel, as well as seasonal fruits, are served in post-siesta snacks or late at night during a game of cards.

Practical Dwellings

In building his house, the farmer is more concerned with practical needs than with beauty. The dwelling is built of such local materials as bamboo, wood, straw, and mud. Even bricks and tiles are baked of clay dug up from the rice fields. The walls and partitions are made of woven bamboo, over which is plastered soft mud. The roofs are covered with a thatch of palm leaves.

In the center room of the main building, which has either three or five rooms, the ancestor's altar occupies the place of honor. Even in the poorest household there is an impressive display of candlesticks, incense-burners, tapestry scrolls, and a shrine containing the ancestral tablets. These bear the names of the omnipresent ancestors—up to the fourth generation—who witness all that is happening in the family.

In addition to the main living quarters, which are constructed in the shape of the Chinese character for "gate" or of an inverted U, and which are reserved for grandparents, parents, and children, there may be separate quarters for servants and farmhands if the household is prosperous. If there are no separate servants' quarters, there will at least be shelters for the water buffaloes, farm equipment, and reserves of grain. Behind the cow pen there are a pig sty and a chicken coop. Surrounding the house is the familiar wall of greenery—groups of banana trees, areca palms rising above the gray thatched roofs, guava trees, mango trees, and the inevitable tall bamboos—to screen the occupants from curious eyes.

In the yard by the kitchen there is frequently a huge brick tank for storing rain water. At the back of each house there is very often a small vegetable garden and sometimes a little pond where children and adults bathe and wash their clothes and dishes.

A Colorful Environment

Other ponds and lakes, abounding in fish, are scattered within the village boundaries; and in front of the *dinh*, a combination of temple and community center, it is not uncommon to see a lotus pond with beautiful, fragrant flowers and large, round leaves.

The village gates are sometimes surmounted by watchtowers. At the approach of strangers, dogs of every size and color—whom people let run loose in the narrow village paths—start barking. Woe to the unwary stranger, for at times the dogs are really ferocious.

Inside the thick bamboo separating the surrounding farmlands from the emerald-like island that each village resembles, are labyrinthine paths that wind among more hedges of bamboo and cactus, and that take the visitor past the schoolhouse, the temple, and the *dinh*.

In the *dinh*, housewives offer prayers and victuals to the guardian spirit, the *thanh hoang*, and ask for his good will and protection against natural disasters. The *thanh hoang* may be a celestial spirit or merely a common human being who happened, a long time ago, to die an unnatural death. In the quiet village, the schoolhouse resounds to the voices of children reciting their lessons, and from the curved-roofed temple come the monks' monotonous prayers, marked by the rhythmic beat of a wooden instrument called the *mo*.

In the middle of the village there is possibly a market, where uncovered loads of fresh vegetables, baskets of grain and peanuts, and trays of such things as fish, meat, salt, sugar, and tobacco are displayed. And if one goes riding in the Vietnamese countryside, one will see every five or six miles a roadside market place consisting of a few dilapidated stalls. Unlike the village markets, these are only opened on certain days of the lunar month: for instance, on the first, the eleventh, and the twenty-first.

Inexpensive Clothing

Clothing is not a large item in the budget of the Vietnamese farmer. A suit consists of a pair of loose, low-crotched trousers, a long-sleeved blouse buttoned in front and resembling a pajama top, and a long tunic buttoned on the right-hand side. The men usually wear a turban and a pair of sandals that look like slippers but have no counters. For everyday use the gown is omitted, and people who labor in the fields add a conical-shaped hat made of woven leaves to protect their heads from the hot tropical sun or the spring rain. Color schemes are simple—people dye their clothes black or brown. But to her mud-colored outfit, a country belle may provide a gay constrast by adding a vermillion and bright-green sash. Materials are invariably of cotton or hemp; for winter, the clothing may have a layer of kapok quilted in between the layers of fabric.

Some of the peasant women wear full skirts instead of trousers. Shoes have little use when one must work knee-deep in the leech-infested mud of the rice fields or walk in the rain on the soaked, muddy ground. Then, too, few people can afford them.

Simple Entertainment

Unlike his Western counterpart, the Vietnamese farmer knows no Sunday at all. Indeed, farm life is so intense that there is not a moment of the year when some kind of work is not going on. Plowing, harrowing, sowing the seeds, transplanting the rice seedlings, weeding, irrigating—every operation is carried out by hand and with the most rudimentary tools, yet attended to with utmost care and patience.

The workday begins when the cock crows. After a hasty breakfast, the peasant family works continuously in the fields until noon. Then they stop to have a heavy lunch, to talk, to joke, to smoke, and to take a nap in the shade of a banyan tree. Afterward, they continue working until late in the afternoon.

When evening comes and the peasants begin to return home, there are few more peaceful sights than that of a young boy riding astride a huge, sluggish water buffalo, the beast walking slowly down the familiar homeward path after a full

As women transplant rice in a flooded field, a young man hands them bundles of plants.

(*Photo: Pham Van Mui*)

day's work. The sub-teenage herdsman may lie down on the animal's back to look at the twilit sky, to play his bamboo flute, or to watch the moon rise above the graceful bamboos.

After dinner, those children who are lucky enough to go to school may do their homework by the light of a smoky castor-oil lamp. Others may stay up to hear their grandparents tell them fabulous tales that have been handed down for generations. The story-telling and the high-pitched conversation, filled with candid humor, continue while the women are busy grinding the rough rice in the polisher or pounding the ground rice in the stone mortar.

Day in and day out, year in and year out, rain or shine, the Vietnamese farmer, his wife, and his children labor untiringly and unrelentingly. Entertainment is rare. On special occasions, an itinerant troupe may stop in the village and give a few colorful performances in the *dinh*. The repertoire is invariably composed of historical plays in which the forces of good (symbolized by a loyal mandarin, a virtuous widow, a faithful lover) always prevail, to the delight of the enthusiastic, betel- and sugarcane-chewing audience. Festivities with such diversions as chess games, card games, buffalo fights, and cock fights are reserved for the New Year—the Tet—when every penny saved through hard work during the year is spent on food, clothing, and gambling.

Indeed, the celebrations go on for a whole month, amidst the bang of firecrackers, as the peasants bid farewell to the old year and welcome the new springtime, which brings new life to the entire village.

Harvest time is a season of festivities too. Then the village again comes alive, as children run to and fro with their mouths full of candy, and as all the inhabitants busy themselves with winnowing and threshing the precious grain. The animals, too, receive special attention, for additional rations are given the piglets, ducklings, and buffalo calves.

Hopeful Life

A life of industry, thrift, and austerity is the common lot of the Vietnamese farmer. Nature is sometimes merciless when she unleashes the river waters against dikes and thus destroys crops, livestock, and human beings. But, between famines, the Vietnamese farmer is always happy and hopeful for the best. Children work hard in anticipation of a rice cake, a period of free time during which they can shoot marbles at the foot of a red-blossomed kapok tree, a chance to fly their kites in the summer breeze, an opportunity to sing their favorite songs, and a break when they can ride the water buffalo and enjoy the moonlight. Young men and women work hard in the hope that their parents will permit them to marry those with whom they have fallen in love during an alternating song contest held the previous month.

Even the old people—who must stay home to weave baskets, make hammocks, and tend babies, thus leaving the harder chores to their children and grandchildren—symbolize the forbearance of the Vietnamese peasant, who lives with a fervent hope in the morrow of the land, in ancestral rites, and in age-old traditions of peace and harmony.

"THE DIEN BIEN PHU STATE FARM," BY *Do Xuan Sang* (in *Vietnam Advances*, October, 1959)

One of the articles of faith for a Communist regime is the value, both economic and social, of the collectivization of agriculture. In North Vietnam, the government pressed the implementation of a land-reform law as soon as the Geneva agreements brought peace. Peasant resistance to the violence and disruption accompanying the land redistribution led to a "peasant revolt" in the fall of 1957. Since then, the Democratic Republic of Vietnam (DRV) has moved cautiously to urge peasants to join cooperatives at all levels, for food production and marketing, but has not begun large-scale collectives like those in China. And to run the show-case state farms, the government has prudently used the army, a source of reliable manpower. Below is an article from a Hanoi magazine describing the inception and workings of such a state farm, which bears the prestigious name of the DRV's great military victory over the French, Dien Bien Phu. Note the references to minority peoples, help from abroad, and the importance accorded to relations between the soldier-farmers and local population. Remember that this, like other articles published in the North, has passed government censorship and thus reflects an official attitude.

Dien Bien Phu valley, which, on May 7, 1954, saw the capitulation of the best French colonial troops, under the command of General Christian de Castries, stretches on either side of the Nam Rom River, along roughly 15 kilometers from Him Lam Che Phai to Pom Coc. Its width varies between 4 and 5 kilometers, and the area of arable land can be estimated at 5,000 hectares, only just over half of which has been cultivated since the events of 1954. The rest consists of grassy hills and land not yet entirely cleared of mines. (The minefields laid by the French Expeditionary Corps were so dense and the mines so difficult to dislodge that the French engineering corps captain responsible for the job was killed —so it was said—while he was inspecting his own work.)

At the beginning of 1958, a Vietnam People's Army unit that had valiantly contributed to the Dien Bien Phu victory was instructed to return to the area to work the land that had remained fallow. Enormous difficulties awaited the unit. Mine-clearing over wide stretches could only be done slowly, at the cost of great effort and sometimes, too, at the cost of human lives.

For the first six months after their return to Dien Bien Phu, the victors of 1954 were short of everything. As during the long and painful War of Resistance, they had to ask the inhabitants for shelter and to feed themselves with sticky rice and dried fish. Vegetables were scarce; ordinary rice, which had to be brought from the delta over a distance of 500 kilometers, was distributed only to those who were ill or as special rations on festival days. For work in the fields, farming implements and draft animals, as well as seeds, existed only in limited quantities.

But the qualities of endurance and high combativeness of the Vietnam People's Army soldiers overcame all the difficulties. The soldiers turned farmworkers conscientiously carried out the directives they had received from the Party and the government: "To make the Northwest their new village and the state farm their new family." They cleared and put under cultivation vast stretches of land; at the same time, they built their own dwellings, started vegetable gardens, and raised cattle. The local population did their best to help them. The Thai minority, after having sheltered them, lent them farming implements and draft animals. The Meo minority gave them —in exchange for ordinary rice—paddy seeds for sowing on high peaks, suitable for dry rice fields.

International solidarity also played a part. The brotherly peoples of the socialist countries made gifts of agricultural machines to the former fighters of Dien Bien Phu. K.D.35 tractors bearing the trademark "Bocsa Rumana 1956" and Soviet D.T.54 tractors produced in Kharkov made their appearance on the cleared fields, not long before overrun with eighteen-ton U.S. tanks parachuted by the Americans and destined for their allies, the French colonialists. A delegation of Chinese agricultural experts came to Dien Bien Phu on December 13, 1958, bringing seeds, young plants, and, above all, their valuable experience in matters of land-clearing.

Officially formed on April 14, 1958, the Dien Bien Phu state farm grew rapidly in an atmosphere of patriotic emulation and international mutual aid. It had its first success in October of the same year: 148 tons of dry rice were harvested over a newly-exploited area of 200 hectares.

The end-of-year balance sheet included, in addition, the following results: the building of dwellings, hangars for the machines, and granaries; the setting up of herds of buffalo, oxen (brought from the delta), goats, and pigs; experimental growing of industrial plants such as camphor trees, lacquer trees, coffee plants, and rubber trees. Orange trees from Bo Ha (Bac Giang) and apple and pear trees from China became well acclimatized at Dien Bien Phu. Kitchen gardens provided abundant vegetables, which substantially improved the workers' meals.

The state farm set up an ice-making factory, a confectioner's, and a canteen where *pho* (Vietnamese noodle-and-beef soup) is sold on market days. It also installed a hairdresser's, a tailor's, and a photographer's for the needs of its members and the local population.

Life at Dien Bien Phu became pleasant to the point where the question arose of bringing the farmworkers' wives and children, so that the farm was for them a large and real family. Even young girls from Hanoi volunteered for agricultural work at Dien Bien Phu.

In this valley, where a few years before the crash of cannons and machine-guns had prevailed, the clear voices of women singing were heard at the end of work hours. The farmworkers and newly-arrived women farmworkers formed football and volley-ball teams and a song-and-dance ensemble that won a prize at an artistic contest organized by the Military Command of the Northwest Autonomous Zone.

Vis-à-vis the local population, the Dien Bien Phu state farm returned the benefits received by actively pushing forward the agricultural cooperation movement in the Thai, Meo, and Xa communities. At present, the administrative district of Dien Bien Phu, which stretches from Tuan Giao to the border of Laos, has nineteen agricultural cooperatives; the Dien Bien Phu valley alone has fourteen. Every one of these cooperatives received warm and disinterested aid from the state farm. The Chien Dong cooperative—the first to be formed—had its fields worked by tractors driven by mechanics from the farm. How great was the young Thai girls' joy on seeing these "steel buffaloes" coming to lighten their work and, seated on the backs of these "animals," the same young men who, five years before, had delivered them from shameful captivity in colonialist concentration camps.*

The state farm is going to extend its activities; 400 hectares

* At the end of 1953, the French colonialists concentrated the whole population of Dien Bien Phu in two camps at Long Nhai and Co My. Of 9,000 internees there, 2,200 died.

have been put under cultivation in 1959; 900 will be in 1960. Besides the paddy for feeding people, industrial plants—especially coffee plants—will enrich the valley. The mountains of Dien Bien Phu will gradually yield their treasures in valuable wood and minerals; and the sulphur spring at Pac Nam, south of Hong Cum, will be a suitable place for a sanatorium. The herds of cattle are increasing so rapidly that it will be necessary to set up new pasture grounds on the mountain slopes along the valley and, later, on the opposite side.

During this time, the agricultural cooperation movement is gaining in width and depth among the local population. At the end of 1960, the cooperatives will include 60 to 70 per cent of the Thai, Meo, and Xa families, according to the local plan; but we can be sure that the plan will be exceeded.

A new battle of Dien Bien Phu—the battle for production and close unity among the Vietnamese Thai, Meo, and Xa minorities in the building of socialism in North Vietnam—has begun and is entering a decisive phase. It can only end in victory.

"MIRACLE RICE COMES TO VIETNAM"

(excerpts from *Vietnam Magazine*, 1968 and 1969)

One of the perennial problems facing Asian nations is the difficulty of producing enough rice to feed the ever expanding population. Although South Vietnam has been a traditional rice-surplus area, exporting rice to the rest of Vietnam and abroad, wartime conditions have sharply curtailed rice production, and the South, too, has become a deficit area. This article describes successful attempts to increase rice production through the development of hybrid rice. It appeared in a publication of the Vietnam Council on Foreign Relations, and its optimistic tone may in part reflect the pro-government position of the organization.

For more than 5,000 years, Asia has been growing and eating rice. The earliest known records show Chinese wading through the water of their rice paddies around 3,000 B.C., tossing in handfuls of seeds, invoking the spirits' help for a good crop, and waiting for the harvest, seven to nine months later.

From West Pakistan to Japan, more than 1 billion Asians, with widely different forms of government and different religions, languages, and traditions, all grow the same crop and eat the same food—rice.

Not long ago, most of these countries had some of their

Newly planted rice — a rice field also provides edible frogs, fish, and ducks.

rice crop left over for export at the end of each year's harvest. In less than a decade, rice production increased by 25 per cent. Yet Asia no longer exports rice. City-dwellers in rice-growing countries are going hungry.

Why? Because 1 million rice-eaters are born each week. The supply of rice is no longer equal to the demand. Asia is steadily losing the race between food and population.

At one time, South Vietnam produced enough rice to export a million tons a year after feeding its own people. As recently as 1963, it was able to export 323,000 tons of rice. But the war has left its mark, and South Vietnam now imports nearly 80 per cent of its rice. These statistics of shortage are reflected in nearly every country of Asia.

In all countries the rice crop depends on the weather. In fields lacking irrigation, too little rain in the rainy season can deprive the rice of the flooded conditions best suited to its growth. Too much rain in the dry season, when the crop is threshed and harvested, can rot the rice before it can be stored or taken to market. With a growing season of seven to nine months, only one crop can be grown each year—there is no chance to make up the loss of a bad crop by quickly planting a new one.

In addition to these hazards of nature, South Vietnam suffers the greater tragedy of two decades of war. Three-fourths of the country's rice paddies are in the Mekong Delta, an area under constant threat from the Viet Cong. In guerrilla warfare, the economy is a major military target, and in the Mekong Delta, the economic target of the Viet Cong is rice.

Wartime conditions make farming difficult and dangerous in the delta and elsewhere in South Vietnam. Transporting the rice to market is equally hazardous. As a result, many rice farmers have abandoned their paddies and moved to the cities, where wartime jobs on construction projects are plentiful and well paid. These new city-dwellers become rice-eaters instead of rice-producers.

Still other rice farmers are serving in the armed forces. Their paddies lie abandoned and are sometimes irreparably damaged by sea water seeping in through broken or unattended dikes.

The efforts of hundreds of specialists working long hours in rice-research institutes have finally produced a hybrid rice seed that may go a long way toward winning the race against famine. The first successful seed is known as IR-8. Its equally promising brother is IR-5.

Hybrid IR-8, the "miracle rice," is insensitive to the number of daylight hours it receives, so it can be grown in any season. Seeds of IR-8 can be planted closer together: Because of the stiff stem, sunlight can penetrate to the bottom leaves. Even more important is its remarkably short growing season —120 days—which enables farmers to plant two or three crops a year instead of one. And one crop of IR-8 yields about three times more rice per hectare than the traditional varieties, so the maximum yield per year can be multiplied nine times.

To get the most benefit from IR-8, the seeds must be planted carefully, weeded and sprayed frequently, and fer-

A farmer in the Mekong Delta uses a modern Japanese-built roto-tiller. (*Photo: AID-Saigon*)

tilized with nitrogen compounds. All this means more work for the farmer. And it risks angering the spirits who play such a large part in his life.

Even if the South Vietnamese do not achieve self-sufficiency by 1970, they will have pioneered the agricultural industrialization of Southeast Asia, pushing forward the most successful agricultural reform program ever carried out in time of war. The rice revolution has begun and cannot be turned back.

"TO DEVELOP FULLY THE PEASANT MASSES' REVOLUTIONARY ENTHUSIASM AND CREATE A STRONG REVOLUTIONARY METTLE IN THE COUNTRYSIDE," BY *Le Duan* (speech delivered at the closing of the fifth session of the party central committee in July, 1961)
(in *Offensive Against Poverty and Backwardness* [Hanoi, 1963])

Along with the elimination of the private sector in the economy, the government of the Democratic Republic of Vietnam has as its goal the transformation of society. Here, the author, the First Secretary of the Central Committee of the Lao Dong (Workers') Party—the ruling Communist Party—frankly discusses the difficulties involved in creating a new role for the peasants in cooperative agriculture. The speech appeared in Nhan Dan (The People), *the Party's daily newspaper, and was then published in a book.*

To build the new productive forces in the countryside *we must rely on the cooperatives and state farms,* primarily

In Vietnamese villages, water buffaloes are traditionally handled by children. (*Photo: Pham Van Mui*)

the cooperatives. This is the key problem in the building of the new productive forces.

A number of comrades do not yet fully realize the meaning of socialist transformation in the countryside. We must see that such transformation is different from the transformation of capitalist industry and trade in town. The latter consists fundamentally in transforming the production relations based on exploitation of man by man, abolishing the exploiting class, and, at the same time, promoting further the development of production on the basis of the great production that exists at present.

As to the socialist transformation of agriculture in our practical situation, it is not mainly to transform the relations based on exploitation, since the exploiting landlord class has been overthrown, and though rich peasants still exist, their acreage land-ownership does not exceed that of the toiling peasants. Therefore, we must transform the whole means of production, turn the scattered individual production into collective production on a big scale, concentrate the labor force and means of production of the poor and well-to-do peasants working individually, in order to *set up a new mode of production having a new labor organization and division.*

In the Soviet Union and the people's democracies in Eastern Europe, cooperativization is linked to the supply of machines and new farm implements. China, Korea, and Vietnam face a new situation: The peasants are organized, but machines are not yet available for agriculture. But the concentration of means of production and reorganization of labor force alone are able to create new productive forces. To create a new productive force through the concentration of labor power, the latter must reach a certain quantity, because only this can create a new division of labor, and thence give rise to a change by leaps and bounds in the productive forces. That is why at present the problem of *enlarging the scale of cooperatives is of great importance.* This is the main link in the strengthening and development of the cooperatives. The lower type of cooperatives—involving from twenty to thirty households—cannot create a new division of labor and cannot clearly manifest their superiority. At present, it is not yet feasible to organize the cooperatives on a wider scale, because technique is still backward and management level low.

Bringing the cooperatives to the scale of the whole hamlet will lead to a new revolutionary upsurge in agricultural development.

When the cooperatives embrace 150-200 households, the problem of management becomes very important. At present, this is their weakest point. In our national economy now, there are three forms of ownership: national ownership, collective ownership, and individual ownership; the first two forms are the principal points. The cooperatives belong to collective ownership: In the management of the cooperatives, *we must grasp their character of collective-ownership* and, at the same time, know how to combine the collective economy of the cooperatives with the additional economy of the coop members' families. At present, the individual ownership created by the additional economy of the coop members' families is still necessary; the additional economy of the coop members' families still supplies 65 per cent of agricultural products to the market. We must not be afraid that it will give birth to capitalism, because it is only an additional economy, the key positions in economy belong already to the state and cooperative economic sector.

URBAN LIFE

"THE URBAN REVOLUTION," BY *François Sully* (in *Newsweek*, January 20, 1969)

The principal commercial and industrial center of South Vietnam is the Saigon-Cholon metropolitan area, with a total estimated population of over 3,200,000. This area is the center for the distribution of products to the country's interior as well as a major port for international and local coastal trade. Other major urban areas with population in excess of 50,000 include Nha Trang, Da Nang, Hue, Ban Me Thuot, Dalat, and Can Tho. Because of the war, hundreds of thousands of refugees have fled the farms for more secure urban areas. The main population centers of the coast and delta region are rapidly expanding, in contrast to the vast central highlands, where the estimated population density is only 50 people per square mile. With the development of coastal transportation and improved security in the delta area, Vietnam's major markets have remained accessible to trade and, based on experience to date, relatively safe for local businessmen.

A war-induced prosperity, reflecting the large U.S. presence in Vietnam, has created a considerable demand for industrial and consumer products. This demand has been filled by a large volume of imports, which in turn has generated a

A modern Vietnamese woman drives her Japanese motorbike through the traffic in Saigon.

(*Photo: Associated Press*)

major portion of the government's revenues. The number of firms producing import substitutes has expanded in recent years, but the deficit remains large. While imports run at approximately $800 million a year, exports barely reach $100 million.

Americans still tend to think of South Vietnam as a land of peasants and paddy fields, and, in the early days of the U.S. involvement, so it was. Less than a decade ago, 85 per cent of the Vietnamese lived in the countryside. But today it is quite a different story. South Vietnam has become more urbanized than Canada or the Soviet Union. And although no one really knows how many Vietnamese now live in the country's swollen cities, some estimates run as high as 50 per cent.

Transformation

"Often we visit a hamlet that we thought was under Viet Cong control—and we find it empty," John Paul Vann, a retired U.S. Army colonel who is now a senior civilian adviser, told me recently. "Its population has been added to the 3 million Vietnamese farmers who have taken the trail to the cities in the past three years." Of those who have left the countryside, perhaps a million and a half fled to the cities as refugees to escape the ceaseless warfare that has ravaged their rural homes. But at least a million and a half more have been lured to the cities by the employment at U.S. bases, where they can earn as much as five times what they can command anywhere else in South Vietnam. "Because of this mass migration," says a Vietnamese engineer, "our situation borders on the schizophrenic. Our feet are deeply rooted in an agrarian and traditional past—and our hands firmly resting on an electric rice-cooker."

Urban services, frail to begin with, have all but collapsed under the impact of peasants flowing into plywood shantytowns where empty artillery shells are used as stoves and napalm containers are fabricated into family pots and pans. In Saigon, which has quintupled in size to 3 million people over the past decade—and now has one of the world's highest density ratios of 12,740 persons per square mile—there are only seventy-one garbage trucks. And last month [December, 1968] Premier Tran Van Huong, faced with an unpaid gasoline bill for the city's buses, simply shut down the capital's transportation system.

Curiously enough, the headlong rush to the cities has hurt the guerrillas more than it has the Saigon Government. One reason is that fewer able-bodied peasants are left in the countryside for the Viet Cong to recruit. Along the Cambodian border, the guerrillas have had to replace scarce human ammunition-bearers with trucks, which—besides being more expensive—are more vulnerable to U.S. air strikes. In once densely populated rural regions, the shortage of men has led the Viet Cong to fill their ranks with young women, who now account for 30 per cent of the village guerrilla units. What's more, the National Liberation Front has been forced to rely on North Vietnamese troops to maintain its military presence in some villages. Remarks John Paul Vann: "We inadvertently stumbled on the solution to guerrilla warfare—urbanization."

The implications of this "solution," however, are grave. For one thing, with only 3 per cent of the Vietnamese work force employed in local industry, the cities are completely dependent on the war for their economic survival. "The greatest industry of this land," admits one Vietnamese economist, "is catering for U.S. Army mess halls and laundering GI fatigues." Moreover, the only men who are trained to run an urbanized society—South Vietnam's civil servants—have almost all been drained off for the war effort. "To build a million-man South

A white *ao dai* over trousers is the uniform of Gia Long Lyceum, an exclusive school for the daughters of Saigon's elite.

Vietnamese army," says a U.S. civil affairs expert in Saigon, "We've stripped teachers, engineers, and administrators from the civil service. This general mobilization is a tragedy."

Theories

On top of all this, the Vietnamese Government is doing little to deal with its urban problems on the optimistic theory, as one American social scientist charges, "that if conditions are bad enough, the squatters will gladly go home when the war is over." But things are not likely to work out that way. "Once they've seen the glamour of the cities," says a U.S. official, "they'll take a shack with television in a slum rather than ten acres of rice in Dullsville."

Meanwhile, the fabric of Vietnamese life is being steadily destroyed. In Phan Rang Province, 170 miles northeast of Saigon, for example, the U.S. Air Force built an airstrip amid lush vegetable gardens and fields in the fond hope of having a convenient supply of fresh cucumbers, tomatoes, and watermelons for its mess halls. Instead, the farmers in the area deserted their fields to live in a nearby shantytown and to work as day laborers. And one Vietnamese newspaper recently lamented: "All our former newsboys have given up their jobs to become pimps or pickpockets."

Future

In the long run, the economic imbalance between an increasingly urban South Vietnam and a predominantly rural North Vietnam—along with all the social disparities that this entails—may make eventual reunification even more difficult than it now appears. It is also hard to foresee a viable future for a reunited Vietnam after the war without a continuing infusion of U.S. aid. Even the National Liberation Front (NLF) negotiating team in Paris acknowledges this fact when it says that it would be willing to accept U.S. aid in a coalition government.

But perhaps the most significant consequence of the forced-draft urbanization but not commensurate industrialization of South Vietnam is its revolutionary implications. "Our cities are social parasites which produce nothing and import everything," warns one South Vietnamese observer. "The cities are potential time bombs for postwar Vietnam. And we are manufacturing them."

"HOI AN: A TOWN THAT REMAINED VIETNAMESE," BY *Le Trang* (in *Saigon Daily News*, July 2, 1968)

This article briefly describes the struggle of a Vietnamese town to maintain its indigenous identity when faced with the ravages of war and a massive infusion of foreign personnel bringing a different way of life and alien values. If this town, as the author asserts, has remained "Vietnamese," even he admits that the young people leave it; it is the older generation, then, that clings to its identity.

Hoi An, sometimes called Faifoo on old French maps, is one of the very few Vietnamese towns that has not suffered changes. Although there are American and Korean troops stationed in the Quang Nam provinces, there are no snack bars and no foreigners in Hoi An. This capital city of Quang Nam province has preserved its ancient aspect, with low houses, narrow streets, and an idle way of life. American cigarettes, tinned beer, canned food, and a few Honda motorcycles cannot change the habits of the people who were born and grew old there.

Hoi An history dates back to the nineteenth century, when the first foreign traders came to Vietnam to sell and buy goods. It was once a prosperous part of ancient Vietnam, and the traces of Japanese, Chinese, and some European merchants still remain.

"This town is too old for young people to live in," a Buddhist monk at one of the five pagodas there sadly told me. "Young people leave for Danang or Saigon, where they can study and make a living. Many have forgotten their home town" he said.

But even if the young people do not forget their town, it is not easy for them to go home very often. It usually takes a passenger bus three hours on peaceful days to cover a distance of about 30 kilometers from Hoi An to Danang city. The road, partly damaged by mines and heavy traffic, is often closed because of sabotage. As a consequence, commodity prices in Hoi An are much higher than in Danang, where the cost of living is already very high.

Most houses have shelters that usually occupy one-fourth of the living spaces. At nightfall people begin to worry, because the town has been the constant target for ground and mortar attacks. As the town is small, people always have the impression that every mortar shell or rocket has exploded next door.

An officer who has not spent one night at home since the 1968 Tet offensive told me that he could judge the situation around the town by watching the market. "When there are fewer people gathering, I know that the guerrillas are nearby."

"STREET VENDORS OF THE CITIES," BY *Nguyen Cuu Giang* (in *Viet My*, June, 1961)

In Saigon, as elsewhere in the urban centers of Asia, much of life is transacted in the streets. Street vendors play an important role in "convenience" marketing and provide a colorful note for the foreigner. As homeless refugees crowd the streets of many towns in the South, both buying and selling in the streets have intensified and provided a means of earning a livelihood for many, as well as a way of obtaining food and services. Viet My *is a monthly published in Saigon by the Vietnamese American Association.*

Perhaps one of the most interesting characteristics of Saigon is that it abounds in various kinds of street vendors. Most of them sell food in the form of delicious Vietnamese delicatessen and sweets. Since the people of this country have developed the inveterate habit of eating between meals, we assume these sidewalk restaurateurs are well patronized and that their small businesses provide them with adequate gains.

The bread vendor might wake you up early in the morning with his cry when he passes by your window; the little Chinese might disturb your siesta by tapping wildly on a sonorous piece of bamboo with a wooden stick—his way of announcing the approach of his father's *hu tieu* (vermicelli) cart, but there isn't anything you can do about it, and you have to adjust yourself to the local way of life.

No less than forty kinds of street vendors work hand in glove with one another to prevent your stomach from staying

Cholon District in Saigon. The canal, intended for drainage and small boats, has become an open sewer, in which children swim and women launder clothes. (*Photo: Pham Van Mui*)

empty for long. In this article we propose to tell you about the most popular ones, whose disappearance from our towns would bring about disastrous effects on the happiness of the Vietnamese.

1. Let us consider the rice-cake (*banh bo*) vendor first.

Banh bo is made of rice flour, leaven, and sugar. The dough is set in a mold and steam-cooked. As the temperature of the water goes up, the piece of dough spreads out in a crawling way to fill the mold, while tiny eyes appear in the cake. *Banh bo* is offered in triangular pieces along with doughnuts. Vietnamese doughnuts take the shape of a beret(*banh-tieu*) or a shin-bone (*gia cha quay*).

Sometimes a lady colleague precedes him by twenty minutes

on his schedule, but she doesn't present much competition to him because on his two-wheeler he can cover a larger area than she can on foot, handicapped as she is with two baskets hanging at either end of a bamboo yoke, which she poises on her right shoulder. Surprisingly enough, her voice can reach much deeper notes than her male counterpart's. In the evening, its monotony sends you to sleep. I wonder how, with such a voice, she can keep people awake long enough to sell them anything at all.

2. Glutinous rice (*xoi*) vendors:

Xoi is prepared with a variety of rice (*nep*), which is stickier than the variety consumed at an ordinary meal in Vietnam. *Xoi* should always be cooked in steam, except when you want to make glue. It can be served either on a piece of green banana leaf with grated coconut and a mixture of sugar, salt, and grilled sesame, or in a plate with a piece of roast chicken on the side. It might be interesting to note that there are practically no men in the *xoi* business. In large cities, *xoi* is the most popular breakfast for laborers, clerks, and students. Main reason: cheapness. In the country, it constitutes the second breakfast for farm hands in general and rice transplanters in particular. The latter always work in groups of ten,

Vietnamese children play with pebbles. Round marbles are rarely used.

(*Photo: Pham Van Mui*)

twenty, or more. They sing while working in the flooded rice-land, and at about seven o'clock, at the farther end of the dike leading to the field, appear two or three little boys who bring the day's second breakfast, steaming hot *xoi* cooked with green beans and coconut milk. This meal is included in the pay and everyone expects it to be decent.

3. *Che thung* vendors:

As with the *xoi* market, the *che thung* business admits no male vendor. All dealers are women.

Che thung is a very thin marmalade made of green beans (*dau xanh*), lotus seeds, translucent noodles (*bot khoai*) and vermicelli (*bung tau*), and Chinese cherries (*trai tao*) cooked in a deep mixture of water and extract of coconut. Customers generally prefer cane sugar to beetroot sugar.

A bowl of sweet and warm *che thung* is a popular nightcap here. You might not be hungry, but if the voice of the woman vendor sounds clear and rich, she has the right to be called in to serve you a bowl of *che thung*, and if her manners are good and her conversation pleasant, you might be inspired to ask your housemaid and your cook to join you at your own expense. All things considered, if a girl doesn't have a pleasant voice, she had better not try to sell *che thung*.

4. Half-hatched-duck-eggs (*Hot vit lon*) vendors:

Half-hatched eggs are offered hard boiled and should be eaten while they are still hot. Relish the duckling and the yoke, and remember, do not throw away the juice! For seasoning, use pepper, salt, and a few sweet-smelling herbs.

You can identify the vendors easily. They all carry a basket full of rice husk, in which the eggs are kept warm. They work in populous districts, public gardens, and in front of temples where, in the evening, theatrical troups perform and other delicacy vendors like to gather. *Hot vit lon* is a good intermission snack for a number of spectators who, squatting in front of the vendor, chase the duckling down their throats with a shot of burning rice wine.

5. Meat Balls (*Nem nuong*) vendors:

Delicious meat balls (usually pork) broiled on live charcoal, *nem nuong* attracts customers by the fat that drips on the fire and changes to an appetizing smoke. The balls are larger than the thumb but never reach the size of the big toe.

6. Soup vendors:

To make a bowl of *pho* (beef soup) take a handful of rice noodle (*banh pho*), put it in a large bowl. Cover the top of the heap with small pieces of raw beef and slices of onion. Pour boiling beef consommé on top and serve with a slice of lime and sweet-smelling herbs. The quality of the broth determines the quality of the soup.

The *pho* vendor pushes his cart slowly from one street corner to another. He yells, "*Pho*!" When he crosses, he might block the street for a while, but please forgive him. He doesn't mean to delay you. It is just that his cart is heavy and there are no ball-bearings in its wheels.

Pho can perhaps be named the most popular breakfast in Vietnam. I do not know of anyone in this country who dislikes a bowl of steaming *pho* followed by a cup of good coffee. *Pho* is also a snack you can have at any time of the day. Twenty years ago, it was introduced to South Vietnam by North Vietnamese immigrants. When it made its debut here, it had to fight for living space with its powerful Chinese counterpart, *hu tieu*. The main difference between *pho* and *hu tieu* lies in the fact that beef, the meat used to prepare *pho*, does not enter into the preparation of *hu tieu*. The Chinese who cook *hu tieu* prefer pork, shrimp, and crab meat and add bean sprouts to their list of ingredients. The odds were against *pho*, because at that time *hu tieu* was enjoying a monopoly over Southern stomachs. *Pho* fought and gained ground little by little. Today, *pho* has as many customers as *hu tieu*, perhaps more, with the refugees from the North, and *pho* vendors make as good a living as *hu tieu* vendors. The South Vietnamese are well taken care of indeed.

RELIGION

"A COMPLEX MIXTURE OF MANY FAITHS," BY *François Sully*

Confucianism, Buddhism, and Taoism, which historically came into Vietnam from China, influenced and were influenced by even older folk beliefs about spirits and supernatural powers still present in the religious expression of the people. Confucianism, as a formal doctrine, remained mainly the province of the educated scholar-bureaucracy, itself formed on the Chinese model. Taoism, realtively neglected by the educated, in time degenerated from its original philosophical sophistication into popular superstition and magic. Buddhism, with its advanced ethics, coherent explanation of human suffering, and promise of individual salvation, gained adherents on all levels of society and became the dominant popular faith of the country, which it remains today.

Christianity was introduced by Catholic missionaries in the sixteenth century, and its growth was fostered under French rule. Today, about 10 per cent of the people are Christians, mostly Roman Catholics, who constitute sizable minorities in both North and South.

In recent years, religious sects borrowing their ethics mainly from Buddhism and Christianity have known an astonishing development in South Vietnam. The Hoa Hao sect, which counts some two million followers in the Mekong Delta, is a

South Vietnam has no state religion, and representatives of major faiths are dutifully invited to government functions. At the top (*left to right*), a Confucian scholar, a Buddhist head monk, and the Catholic Bishop of Saigon attend an official gathering in Saigon. Below that, two Cao Dai dignitaries confer in front of a temple in Tay-Ninh. At the bottom right is the funeral of a Confucian scholar. Here, a Vietnamese cabinet minister holds a portrait of his deceased father while a geomancer directs the burial procedures. At the bottom left, Buddhist Venerables leave a ceremony at Vien Hoa Dao, the national Buddhist shrine in Saigon.

reformed Buddhism without clergy. The Cao Dai, with one million followers throughout the nation, seeks universal truth through the unification of many forms of religion.

"REQUEST OF THE MANDARINS AGAINST THE CHRISTIANS," *August,* 1826 (in Georges Taboulet, *La Geste Française en Indochine* [Paris, 1955]), translated by *Marjorie Weiner Normand*

Christianity came to be viewed with hostility by the mandarinate, the ruling class in Vietnam, which saw in it a threat to the imperial social structure. By the eighteenth century, the mandarins also considered the missionaries an entering wedge for European military penetration and territorial acquisition. Persecution of Catholics lasted until the end of the eighteenth century. But a French missionary, Pigneau de Behaine, Bishop of Adran, aided a prince of the Nguyen dynasty to re-unify Vietnam; the Nguyen prince became the Emperor Gia Long, and throughout his reign, French missionaries remained protected. His successor, Emperor Minh Mang, with the active support of his mandarins, tried to rid Vietnam of all missionaries. Below is translated a petition addressed to the emperor by his mandarins, listing their grievances against Christianity and begging his support.

Seized with fear, we bow our heads and present our request. We beg Your Majesty to think about the establishment of a true religion, so that the upper classes and the people could profit. . . . Any religion which seduces and deceives the people is a perverse religion. . . .

This religion [Christianity] is false and contrary to true doctrine. It seduces the people and takes advantage of their simplicity; it uses fear of torment and hell to frighten the weak, and the enjoyment of the pleasures of heaven to attract others. It is on the point of publishing a private calendar. It even has its own tribunals to judge things. Those who follow this religion assemble, offer sacrifices, and worship; thousands of people come and go, to offer homage, as if they were going to visit one of the most important dignitaries of the kingdom. They claim that their cause is divine and it bestows blessings on those who follow it. Since this religion entered the kingdom, thousands of people have followed it in all the provinces. Those who are imbued with this doctrine are animated with a zeal that transports them outside of themselves and causes them to run here and there like madmen.

Followers of this religion do not worship the Spirit of reason; they do not pay reverence to their ancestors . . . they multiply from day to day; they continually build new churches . . . that is why we look to Your Majesty and appeal for correction of all these abuses.

We have examined the code of the prohibitory Chinese laws. There it is written: "All Europeans residing in our kingdom who make a name for themselves and who head a cause to seduce and abuse the good people are guilty of a great crime and deserve to be strangled. As for those who have neither position nor reputation, they must first be imprisoned, and then we will see. Those who have been seduced and profess this religion must be sent as slaves to the barbarians. Those who use captious speech to seduce a multitude of stupid and shameless women, as well as those who extract the eyes of sick people, if they are taken, will be punished in accordance with the gravity of their crime. Furthermore, all civil and military mandarins as well as subordinate officers, who are seen to lack vigilance, will be brought before a great tribunal to be judged."

All these rigorous defenses are very good and valuable to obstruct perverse doctrines. . . . That is why we beg Your Majesty to Publish an edict . . . so that the whole world will know that all Europeans and advocates of the Christian religion, wherever they are, must return to their country. Give them three months for that; after this time, they will be forbidden to stay longer in this country. It is necessary to destroy the churches, burn the religious books, and forbid the people to study this perverse doctrine any longer. If, after three months, a European is found hidden in the kingdom, he who discovers and denounces him will gain all the property of he who concealed the European in his house. In addition, the one who hid him and the village chiefs will be regarded as guilty of a grave crime. If the European continues to hide among the people and they let themselves be seduced by a wicked doctrine to the point where it will be impossible to purify the kingdom of this defilement, then the stranger will be put to death in accordance with the Chinese law. . . .

For us, we are worthless people. . . . Have we acted rightly or wrongly? We raise our eyes to the throne of Your Majesty and beg you to examine this matter.

"PRESIDENT HO CHI MINH'S MESSAGE TO VIETNAMESE CATHOLICS, 1954"

(in *Statements by President Ho Chi Minh After the Geneva Conference* [Hanoi, 1955])

Following the signing of the Geneva agreements on July 20–21, 1954, peace came to a Vietnam divided at the Seventeenth Parallel. But for many Vietnamese, peace brought additional hardships. Hundreds of thousands of North Vietnamese Catholics, terrified by reports that the Democratic Republic of Vietnam (DRV) would persecute them and proscribe their religion, fled South. In this radio broadcast, the President of the DRV attempts to allay these fears and encourage Catholics to come to terms with the government.

During more than eight years of war, airplanes and tanks have burned down many churches and killed quite a number of Catholics. For many years, this is the first time that we celebrate Christmas in peace.

We should have been much happier and more joyful than we are. This is due to the "attitude of a number of Western people who, instead of obeying Lord Jesus's words, behave like those who killed the Lord" (François Mauriac, Catholic member of the French Academy).

Those Western people are the American people and their lackeys, such as Ngo Dinh Diem; they have deceived or coerced a number of Catholics to leave their native country for the South to live there a miserable life. Young men are forced to become soldiers, women are sold to houses of prostitution, the able-bodied have to slave in rubber plantations, boys and girls are sold to be employed as servants.

Thinking of these Catholic citizens' fate is painful to me, it must also be painful to you. I earnestly hope that you will pray, so that the Lord will give protection to those unhappy citizens in their struggle to be sent back to their native places.

I take this opportunity to reiterate that our government sincerely respects freedom of faith. Regarding those Catholic citizens who have been deceived into going to the South, the government has ordered the local authorities to take care of their lands and properties, which are to be restituted to their owners on their return.

On the occasion of Christmas, I convey to you my cordial greetings, and I pray that the Lord blesses all of you.

"CAO DAISM: STATE RELIGION, NATIONAL RELIGION OF VIETNAM," BY *General Tran Quang Vinh* (in Gabriel Gobrun, *History and Philosophy of Cao Daism* [Saigon, 1950])

Of all the politico-military sects that have flourished in South Vietnam in the twentieth century, Cao Daism is the strongest and best organized. It controls its own territory, has a militant army, and has warred in the past against both the French and the Viet Minh. The following article, written by a late commander in chief of the Cao Dai troops, attempts to explain its mystical amalgam of the beliefs of many religions.

Cao Daism is of a spiritual essence. Its creation proceeds from spiritism. Its doctrine and worship were taught to men by the interpreter of the billed basket. Messages came either from the Supreme God, Cao Dai Himself, or such Superior Spirits as Ly Thai Bach, the Chinese poet Ly Tai Pe of the Duong [Tang] dynasty, now become spiritual Pope of Cao Daism. Spirits of European great men, among others,

Victor Hugo [Nguyet Tam Cho'n Nho'n], often intervened to dictate religious precepts in verse.

Cao Daism is an amalgam, a synthesis of existing religions: Confucianism, Taoism, Buddhism, Christianity, and so on. It does not neglect animistic worships and the deification of heroes of the Sino-Vietnamese antiquity.

The architecture of the Den Thanh [Great Temple] that draws the admiration of foreign tourists by its audacious conception and scope, was inspired by the Pope Ly Thai Bach, or Ho Phap Pham Cong Tac, present Superior of Cao Daism, who had the merit of accomplishing the building with very reduced means under the most unfavorable circumstances. It is artistically decorated with all the symbols of the associated religions, legends, and beliefs of the Sino-Vietnamese folklore: This heterogeneous mixture makes of it a monument of great originality. The most characteristic of innovations is the Tower of Saker [Nghinh Phong], whence melodious and enchanting modulations of an invisible chorus mysteriously escape. It is crowned with a fabulous animal, the Dragon Horse [Long Ma] that carries on its back the first signs of the Chinese Zodiac. . . .

The administrative structure is that of a modern state. There are the executive power [Cu'u Trung Dai] the legislative power [Hiep Thien Dai], and the charitable body [Co Quan Phu'oc Thien], distinctive token of the religion. . . .

The Cao Daist regime is fundamentally democratic. Nominations and promotions in the episcopal hierarchy are first submitted to an assembly of faithful [Van Linh] composed of representatives of parishes in the ratio of one delegate per 500 members or fraction thereof. They are then submitted to the Sacerdotal Counsel, the High Counsel, and, finally, the Spiritual Pope Ly Giao Tong.

The Holy See is situated at Tay Ninh, four kilometers from the chief town of the province.

"IN SEARCH OF THE ENEMY OF MAN," BY *Thich Nhat Hanh* (in *Vietnam, Lotus in a Sea of Fire* [New York, 1967])

Buddhism is the major religion of Vietnam. It is combined by many Vietnamese, in a noncompetitive way, with the Confucian doctrine of reverence for ancestors. Buddhist monks pervade Vietnamese society. In recent years, spurred by what they considered persecution of their religion by a Catholic president, Ngo Dinh Diem, they turned to political activism. One of the most electrifying acts of defiance against the Diem regime was the self-immolation of Buddhist monks in 1963.

In this letter to the Rev. Dr. Martin Luther King, a well-known American advocate of nonviolence, a Vietnamese Buddhist monk attempts to explain the religious rationale for self-immolation. The author, Thich Nhat Hanh, is a scholar and a poet. Until he left his country, he was a professor of religion and director of social studies at Van Hanh, the Buddhist university in Saigon. In the summer of 1966, he made a lecture tour of the United States and nine Western European countries, which culminated in an audience with Pope Paul.

The self-burning of Vietnamese Buddhist monks in 1963 is somehow difficult for the Western Christian conscience to understand. The press spoke then of suicide, but, in the essence, it is not. It is not even a protest. What the monks said in the letters they left before burning themselves aimed only at alarming, at moving the hearts of the oppressors, and at calling the attention of the world to the suffering endured then by the Vietnamese. To burn oneself by fire is to prove that what one is saying is of the utmost importance. There is nothing more painful than burning oneself. To say something while experiencing this kind of pain is to say it with utmost courage, frankness, determination, and sincerity. During the ceremony of ordination, as practiced in the Mahayana tradition, the monk-candidate is required to burn one or more small spots on his body in taking the vow to observe the 250 rules of a *bhikshu,* to live the life of a monk, to attain enlightenment, and to devote his life to the salvation of all beings. One can, of course, say these things while sitting in a comfortable armchair; but when the words are uttered while kneeling before the community of *sangha* and experiencing this kind of pain, they will express all the seriousness of one's heart and mind, and carry much greater weight.

The Vietnamese monk, by burning himself, says with all his strength and determination that he can endure the greatest of sufferings to protect his people. But why does he have to burn himself to death? The difference between burning oneself and burning oneself to death is only a difference in degree, not in nature. A man who burns himself too much must die. The importance is not to take one's life, but to burn. What he really aims at is the expression of his will and determination, not death. In the Buddhist belief, life is not confined to a period of 60 or 80 or 100 years: life is not confined to this body: life is universal. To express will by burning oneself, therefore, is not to commit an act of destruction but to perform an act of construction, that is, to suffer and to die for the sake of one's people. This is not suicide. Suicide is an act of self-destruction, having as causes the following: (1) lack of courage to live and to cope with difficulties; (2) defeat by life and loss of all hope; (3) desire for nonexistence.

This self-destruction is considered by Buddhism as one of the most serious crimes. The monk who burns himself has lost neither courage nor hope; nor does he desire nonexistence. On the contrary, he is very courageous and hopeful and aspires for something good in the future. He does not think that he is destroying himself; he believes in the good fruition of his act of self-sacrifice for the sake of others. Like the Buddha in one of his former lives, who gave himself to a hungry lioness that was about to devour her own cubs, the monk believes he is practicing the doctrine of highest compassion by sacrificing himself in order to call the attention of and to seek help from the people of the world.

I believe with all my heart that the monks who burned themselves did not aim at the death of the oppressors but only at a change in their policy. Their enemies are not man. They are intolerance, fanaticism, dictatorship, cupidity, hatred, and discrimination, which lie within the heart of man. I also believe with all my being that the struggle for equality and freedom you lead in Birmingham, Alabama, is not really aimed at the whites but only at intolerance, hatred, and discrimination. These are real enemies of man—not man himself. In our unfortunate fatherland we are trying to plead desperately: do not kill man, even in man's name. Please kill the real enemies of man that are present everywhere, in our very hearts and minds.

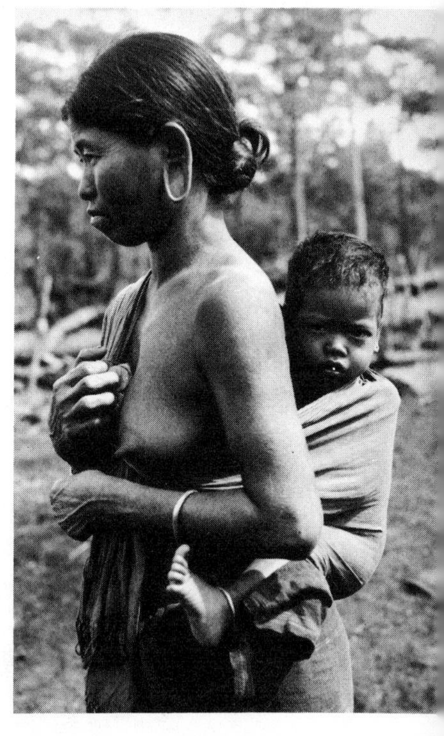

About 700,000 tribesmen occupy the highlands of South Vietnam, representing some twenty different nationalities, each with its own dialect, customs, and geographical area. Above is a fortified tribal village. Some tribal groups have joined the National Liberation Front; others have become Civilian Irregulars under the Saigon government. A third group, known as FULRO, has created a movement pressing for autonomy for the ethnic groups of South Vietnam's highlands. To the right is a woman of the Ma tribe; below is a Montagnard communal long house where a small clan formed by half a dozen interrelated families lives together. (*Photos: JUSPAO-Saigon*)

TRADITIONS, CUSTOMS, FESTIVALS

"ANCESTOR WORSHIP," BY *Pham Lan*
(in *Vietnam Advances,* February, 1958)

Vietnamese honor the spirits of their ancestors with sincerity, without superstition or fanaticism. For them it is a ritual of high moral and social importance. It has been called the true religion of Vietnam, but such a remark confuses religion with ritual. The Cult of the Ancestors is a ritual of filial piety which, in the politico-moral system of Confucius, is the base of all virtues, the foundation of family morals and, consequently, of society and of the state.

The following article was published in a magazine in North Vietnam.

If one were to look inside a Vietnamese house, one would see a big altar, usually placed behind a curtain at the far end of the biggest room. Many religious objects would be seen: incense burners, candlesticks, ivory chopsticks, and small trays for offerings, surrounding a big lacquered board—the tabernacle—with the names of the dead inscribed. Beside the altar hang a little tom-tom and a tiny bell, ready to call back the dead to the family dwelling on anniversaries and traditional festival days.

In families still attached to tradition, big ceremonies are held on these anniversaries. From dawn, the sons, daughters, nephews, nieces, grandsons, and granddaughters of the deceased gather at the home of the latter's eldest son [the man in the family responsible for the expenses of this particular function], bringing with them offerings of every kind: fruit, meat, chicken, glutinous rice, and the ever indispensable "money for the dead." The latter is of many kinds: ingot-shaped money made of bamboo wrapped in colored paper, or notes of very thin homemade paper with a square gilded spot in the middle, or even "bank notes" bearing the inscription "paper money for the Kingdom of the Dead" (*Giay bac Am Phu*). It is said that it is necessary to burn this money to give the dead the funds to live in the other world and to come home on anniversary days. The more money that is burned the happier the ancestral spirits will be.

When the entire family have arrived, they go and visit the grave of the dead person in honor of whom the ceremony is held. New earth is played on top of the grave, the weeds, removed from around it, and then incense is burned to invoke the soul to the family dwelling for the religious function to follow.

At about noon, the altar is already illuminated with candlelight and fragrant with the perfume of burned incense: trays of food to be offered to the family ancestors are displayed on a sacred table.

With the little tom-tom sounding and the bell chiming, the heir, on behalf of the family, steps forward on to the rush mat spread in front of the altar. He kneels down, joins his hands before his mouth and recites prayers. The name of the deceased is pronounced in a low whisper, thus showing the respect of the descendants for their ancestor. At the same time, all the dead of the family up to the fifth generation are invited to come and participate in the feast.

The ceremony ends when all the men and women have

prostrated themselves before the altar. The manner of prostration differs between the men and the women. The ladies sit down, join their hands in front of their chests, and slowly bend down to the mat. The men, on the other hand, raise their clasped hands, kneel and lower their heads to the ground. These motions are called *lay* in Vietnamese, and in each ceremony four *lays* should be made before the altar for the departed ancestors.

Afterward, the "money for the dead" is burned in the courtyard, with the family sitting round the fire, shouting with joy when the ashes, due to the hot currents of air, are lifted up and carried away, because, they say, it is a sign that the dead have received their money.

When the ceremony is over, all the members of the family sit down round the tables and enjoy the meal, conversing meanwhile reminiscently of their ancestors.

On the occasion of the Lunar New Year celebrations, all the departed ancestors of the family up to the fifth generation are invited to return home for the festivals.

Formerly, big ceremonies were also held on the fifteenth day of the seventh month of the lunar year, to present the spirits with more clothes and other items such as houses, rickshaws, furniture, and even concubines and servants. These, made out of paper, were burned.

These customs can be traced back thousands of years and have deep roots in the minds of the Vietnamese. According to the teachings of Confucius, one should worship one's ancestors, otherwise one is accused of impiety. As the saying goes, "Impiety is of three kinds, to have no children being the greatest." The meaning of this is that any man who has no sons—the girls being allowed to worship ancestors only in cases where there are no male descendants—is guilty of impiety, because after him there is no one to "smoke incense" for the dead, and the ancestors will have to wander from place to place, living on alms.

Nowadays, the old beliefs and superstitions are waning away; thus, in big cities, the altar is becoming smaller and in some cases nonexistent; but in the countryside, among the peasantry, it still occupies the best place in the house.

"THE TET IN VIETNAM," BY *Professor Pham Gia Trinh* (adapted from his article in *Viet My*, December, 1966)

Tet is Vietnam's biggest celebration of the year. It corresponds to America's Christmas, New Year's, Thanksgiving, and Fourth of July combined. It is a family reunion, a spring festival, a national holiday, and everybody's birthday!

The three-day event announces the new lunar year and the beginning of spring. Like that of Easter, the date for Tet is based on the lunar calendar. It usually occurs in late January or early February. For the Vietnamese, it is a time of solemnity, gaiety, and hope. It is a time to pay homage to ancestors, visit family and friends, observe traditional taboos, and, of course, to celebrate. Tet also is the time to correct faults, forget past mistakes, pardon others for their offenses, and pay debts. To owe money during Tet is considered bad luck. It is a time to come to terms with the past, tidy up the present, and prepare for the future. A happy Tet is the augury for a good year.

This is the time when the Vietnamese people look back on their past, enjoy the present, and look forward to the future. It is truly a comprehensive holiday, and all Vietnamese give it full observance.

Rites and Prohibitions Concerning the Tet

The custom of celebrating the Tet goes back to remote antiquity. Like many other Vietnamese traditions, it was imported from China, probably by the Chinese tribe of the Yueh, who came 4,000 years ago from the banks of the Yang Tse Kiang to settle in the land of the Giao Chi (now North Vietnam). The essence of this custom has been maintained throughout the ages, but its rites have changed, and their original significance gradually has been lost or deformed by officiating priests, so that later generations have often come to repeat words and gestures so transformed that they have lost all meaning. Certain old books on magic sometimes give an idea of what was in the mind of the old master who devised and imposed such and such a proceeding, but, more often, one can only conjecture.

One of the best-preserved rites of the Tet is the celebration of the feast of the djinn of the home, on the twenty-third day of the twelfth month. It gradually lost its original meaning, even in China, and when it was imported into Vietnam, it underwent a profound change in the mind of the people and became merely a sentimental little story.

The same may be said of nearly all the customs concerning the Tet: Originally they were imbued with lofty and precise philosophical significance, although this was always disguised under a poetic parable. However, the incomprehension of later ages brought about such profound transformations and alterations that most of them have degenerated into mere superstitious practices. They should be examined in this light, rather than rejected *en bloc* as beliefs of no value, unworthy of being taken into consideration. Nothing is more moving than the permanence of these rites that are like messages addressed to us by our ancestors from the depths of time.

We do not intend to study all the customs of the Tet in the following lines but merely to single out some of those that are most generally practiced.

The Peachtree Branch and the Story of Than do and Uat luy

One of the most characteristic customs of the Tet consists in buying a flowering branch of the peach tree, which is placed in a vase for the whole duration of the Tet.

Certain villages of Hanoi specialize in the cultivation of peach trees for this purpose, specially on the Great Lake, near the village of Chem. There are firms in Hanoi, however, that have a reputation for manufacturing artificial peachtree branches that exactly resemble real flowers and have the advantage of being much cheaper and lasting the whole year!

Many people imagine that these branches have no other purpose than to add a graceful decoration to Vietnamese homes, and today, in fact, they have no other significance. Originally, however, they had the same effect as the *cay neu* and were used, like them, to protect oneself from the visit of demons. An old Chinese book, the *Kinh so tue thon ky*, lays down that two boards made of peach wood and covered with terrifying drawings of the djinns Than do and Uat luy, should be placed against the door of every house. These boards were called *dao phu* (the talisman in peach wood). The first emperor of the Chinese dynasty of the Ming had them replaced by bands of red paper, covered with the same drawings.

At the same period, these boards were transformed into the graceful branches of the flowering peach tree we know today. As for the djinns Than do and Uat luy, the old book *Phong Tuc Thong* tells the following story about them:

They were two brothers who possessed the marvelous power of seeing demons, even in full daylight, and of exterminating them. Heaven thus entrusted them with the mission of posting themselves in front of houses, chiefly at the time of the Tet, to bar the way to any demons who might make their appearance. They were so feared that it was enough to draw their pictures, with grimacing faces, on sheets of red paper, to frighten away the evil demons forever.

Giao Thua

According to the Chinese astrological calendar, time is circumscribed in revolutions of sixty years, divided into cycles of twelve years, each cycle containing twelve months, and so on. Years and months thus have the same names: there is the year *thin* [Dragon], just as there is the month *thin*; the year *ty* [Serpent], the month *ty*, the day *ty*, the hour *ty*, and so on.

A cycle of twelve years is placed under the sign of twelve supernatural powers [*hanh khien*], some of whom are well disposed and others hard and cruel. On the last night of the year, the power on service passes his office to the new power: It is this passing of service that is known as *giao thua*.

In town and countryside, the head of every family, every mayor (*ly truong*), every mandarin at the head of a province, the king in his capital, and all the pagodas must offer up a solemn sacrifice at the same moment, in thanksgiving to the old power *hanh khien*, and welcome to the new. This ceremony of *giao thua* is performed at midnight, at the moment when the hour of the Pig (*gio hoi*) changes to that of the Rat (*gio ty*) and is carried out with great solemnity. In the old days, it used to be accompanied by noisy and interminable fireworks and the beating of tom-toms. This has given rise to the expression "*Trong keu ran nhu trong giao thua*" ("A rolling of drums comparable to those of the *giao thua*").

It is the custom at *giao thua* for everyone to remain awake till morning, so as to be prepared to welcome in the favorable influences of the New Year. It is amusing to see how, as soon as the first drums of the pagoda announce the passage of the New Year, parents rush to wake up all the children in the house, sitting them up by force, in spite of their cries and grumblings.

The Prohibition on Sweeping

It is strictly forbidden to sweep the house, once the *giao thua* is over, during the first day of the Tet. During the days that follow, sweeping is allowed, but it is absolutely forbidden to gather up the rubbish and throw it away.

This custom also comes from China and the *Phong Tho Ky* tells the following story:

"There used to live in Heaven a young housewife named Bi Tieu, whose duty it was to cook the celestial meals (*thien tao, thien tru*). As she was extremely greedy, she used to take copious samplings of all the dishes she prepared for the master of the universe. One day the latter, in a rage, exiled her to earth, where she was forced to take the form of a broom (*than choi*) so that in future she would pick up only rubbish instead of the delicacies of the heavens.

"She was so ashamed and unhappy in this existence that she sent up a prayer, explaining that she worked unceasingly and never had a day of rest. Heaven was touched and granted her a day of respite on every New Year's Day."

For this reason it is forbidden to touch a broom on that day.

Vietnamese children recite the following riddle: "*Trong nha co mot ba hay la liem*," which means: "What person in the house scrounges all she wants?" The answer, of course, is: "The broom," which picks things up wherever it passes.

This foolish belief is one of those we should do well to suppress, since it in no way contributes to the gaiety or picturesqueness of the Tet and encourages dirtiness.

The same is true of the prohibition to remove household refuse, the origin of which is to be found in another Chinese legend. The book *Suu than ky* relates how a poor wretch of a Chinese named Au Minh was sitting one day near the lake Than Thao and meditating bitterly on his poverty. The djinn of the lake was moved to pity and made him a present of a tiny charm in the form of an animal named Hau. Au Minh was soon extremely rich. One day—it happened exactly on New Year's Day—he fell into a temper and almost crushed the little animal beneath his foot. It disappeared into a heap of rubbish lying in a corner of the house. His owner sought him everywhere but never thought of looking in the very place where he lay hidden. The rubbish was thrown out, and the poor little thing went with it. After this, Au Minh quickly became as poor as he had been before, and since then, it has become a custom never to throw away the household rubbish during the three first days of the year. This would mean, symbolically, that one would be throwing away one's most precious possession.

Canh Loc

One of the customs concerning the Tet has a curious resemblance to a practice taught by the Druids of ancient Gaul, who used to lead the people into the forest on the first day of the year to seek the lucky branches of mistletoe that they would keep for the following twelve months.

The Chinese and Vietnamese are also expected to bring home from their first walk of the New Year a leafy branch, if possible covered with fruit and flowers (*canh loc*). The heavier the branch, the greater will be the riches (*loc*) earned during the coming year.

A *Historic* Banh Chung

Everyone knows how the great chief Nguyen Hue, enthroned under the name of Quang Trung, defied the Chinese of the first Ts'ing dynasty in the Hanoi plain, during the first days of the Tet in the year Ky Dau [1789].

The *Dao khe nhan toai* explains that King Quang Trung was able to enter so easily into Thang Long [Hanoi], thanks to a . . . *banh chung* (rice cake specially made for the Tet). The Chinese, in order to gain the confidence of the Vietnamese population, had given various fairly important posts to Vietnamese who had taken their side or had appeared to do so. It is thus that important army stores had been entrusted to a Vietnamese named Dinh, who was in reality an ardent patriot and resistant.

King Quang Trung desired that the liberation of Thang Long should be brought about by a simultaneous attack by his troops coming from the exterior and by the resistants within. The question was, how to warn Dinh and his men of the day on which the attack was to take place?

As the Tet had just begun, King Quang Trung had the idea of entrusting a few *banh chung* to an old *ong do* [school teacher] named Nguyen Thiep. A message was hidden in one of them, marked by the king's seal and addressed to Dinh, the chief of the resistants.

The result was that, at the moment when Quang Trung's troops arrived at the gates of Thang Long and engaged the battle with the Chinese garrison under Marshal Ton Si Nghi, a tremendous fire broke out in the army storehouses, set alight by Dinh and his men.

Ton Si Nghi, ill-informed, imagined that Quang Trung's troops had already penetrated the capital. In a panic, he ordered his own men to withdraw from the town and gain the far bank of the Red River, so that they should not risk having their retreat cut off. He even forgot his personal papers and his commander's seal, which fell ino the hands of King Quang Trung.

Tet Cung, *or a Delayed Tet*

It is generally supposed that the Tet begins in Vietnam on the first day of the first month of the Sino-Vietnamese New Year. This is true in general, but there is an exception in certain provinces in North Vietnam, where the Tet is celebrated later during the first month. This custom, which is practiced in the provinces of Hadong, Sontay, Thai Nguyen, and so on, dates only from the reign of the Emperor Tu Duc and is thus seventy or eighty years old.

We have heard of an explanation given by certain old men, survivors of this heroic period. Emperor Tu Duc's reign was marked by numerous uprisings and especially by frequent raids by Chinese pirates known as the "Black Flags." These pirates knew that the Vietnamese, like the Chinese, were in the habit of holding sumptuous celebrations for the Tet, and they profited by the occasion to loot, burn, rape, and massacre among the inhabitants of the Upper Delta.

After several years of this treatment, the people got together and decided to adopt the practice of *Tet cung* (delayed Tet). During the days when other Vietnamese were celebrating joyfully, these people would leave their homes and go to hide in the nearby woods and mountains, after burying all their valuables. The pirates, finding nothing to interest them, finished by concluding that the region was so poor that its inhabitants had not even enough to keep the Tet.

A few days later, the villagers would return and hold their feasts in peace, finding their pleasure even greater for the delay. They became so used to this "delayed Tet" that they have kept the custom faithfully ever since.

"GEOMANCY: THE MAGIC ART OF LANDSCAPING" (*Anonymous*)

Many Vietnamese believe that their fortunes can be influenced by the selection of a propitious burial site for a deceased father. The divination of sites favorably influenced by the magnetism of the earth is called geomancy—an Asian science so much ignored in the West that the very word has been omitted by the Encyclopædia Britannica. Old men knowledgeable in this esoteric science are called geomancers: Their services are sought after by heads of states and powerful generals, as well as by scholars who seek to become the great men of their times.

Ngo Dinh Diem, the late President of South Vietnam, paid much attention to the burial site of his father, the mandarin Ngo Dinh Kha, whose grave had the shape of a giant tortoise, the sacred animal of Vietnamese mythology. The magnificent grave was located on the hill of Phu Cam, on the south bank of the Perfumed River in central Vietnam. In his desire to improve the site further, Diem had an architect build a pond in front of the grave, for a stream of water is thought to improve a geomantic site. Unfortunately, the kidney-shaped pond, as designed by the country's most famous young architect, severed the neck of the sacred animal. Shortly afterward, Diem was murdered by his own generals, two of his brothers were killed, and the rest of the Ngo family forced into exile. This is how some Vietnamese explain history.

Magic Landscaping

Geomancy, which inspired the layouts of Rome and Byzantium, is a quasi-science related to astrology and alchemy, a medieval process of transforming something common into something precious. Geomancy is characteristic of the Asian world deeply impregnated by metaphysical beliefs.

Most Vietnamese believe that by the appropriate transformation of a landscape, either the digging of an artificial waterway or the building of an earth mound, one can capture the hidden strength of nature. Some Vietnamese military men conceive strategy as a science related to astrology and geomancy. A general, for example, should never build his camp on a malefic site nor engage in battle on an unfavorable day.

Geomancy has certain negative aspects: One should not trouble the world's order nor the harmony of nature with a house too high, a straight road cutting across the dragon's vein, the drying of a natural pond, the cutting of old trees bringing beauty to a landscape.

Conversely, geomancy also has its positive aspects: Man can conjure evil influences by the construction of a canal or the building of a monument at the critical place of a region. Central Vietnam, for example, contains many sites regarded as propitious by geomancers, a fact perhaps explaining why so many Vietnamese leaders—from Ngo Dinh Diem to Ho Chi Minh—came from that region.

The duties of a geomancer are:

(1) to find the chosen site corresponding to the stars and the constellations governing the world, and then to select the most propitious location. Earth is regarded as the reflection of sacred animals: the phoenix, tortoise, and dragon, who live in Heaven.

(2) to use the geomantic compass very different from a

marine compass. The geomantic compass gives the direction of the two main "winds": The beneficent Blue Dragon wind (*thanh long*) and the White Tiger (*bac ho*), or pernicious wind. The closer one gets to the mouth of the Dragon, the more favorable the site. But it is absolutely necessary to ascertain that the Blue Dragon current flows on the left and that the White Tiger current flows on the right of the privileged site. Only the man of virtue can usefully use geomancy as he is guided by the forces of Heaven.

In ancient Vietnam, an emperor could order the removal of tombs located in auspicious sites, fearing they would give magical strength to the descendants of the buried persons to challenge his own power. These graves were commonly regarded as "the dangerous tombs" by the emperor's courtiers looking after the security of the kingdom. Desecration of their parents' graves was a common punishment for rebels and usurpers of the throne.

Two girls at prayer burn joss sticks in a Saigon temple dedicated to a national hero. Long coils of incense hang from the ceiling.

(*Photo: Pham Van Mui*)

WOMEN IN VIETNAM

"THE INSURRECTION OF THE TWO TRUNG SISTERS," BY *Van Tan* (in *Vietnam Advances* [Hanoi, 1960])

The Trung sisters are Vietnam's best-loved national heroines, and their story of heroism and self-sacrifice is known by all. The article reproduced below is notable not only for its story of the Trung sisters, but also because it appeared in a North Vietnamese publication. The author had no difficulty excoriating the Chinese "feudalists" for oppressing the Vietnamese, despite his government's close alliance with China: Vietnam's long enmity with her northern neighbor is part of the Vietnamese cultural and historical tradition.

The insurrection of the two sisters Trung Trac and Trung Nhi was the first in date in the annals of the struggle waged by Vietnam against the domination of the Chinese feudalists and also the first in date in the process of development of the Vietnamese nation.

In the year 34 of our era, under the Han dynasty, a Chinese governor named To Dinh ruled over the country of Giao Chi, which corresponded roughly to present-day North Vietnam. Our subject country was turned into a land of allegiance by the Chinese court. To Dinh, greedy and brutal, carried out a policy of harsh exploitation and oppression. He forced the population to dive into the depths of the sea for pearl oysters, and to hunt elephants and rhinoceros in the forest for their ivory and horns. . . . A noble of the country at the time had two daughters, Trung Trac and Trung Nhi, both renowned for their bravery and much respected by the people. The two sisters felt a deep hatred for To Dinh.

In the year A.D. 40, To Dinh had Thi Sach, Trung Trac's husband, put to death. She and her sister, Trung Nhi, called on the people to rise up and throw off the foreign yoke. The people won victory after victory. In a short space of time, they liberated sixty-five towns. To Dinh and his men had only just sufficient time to flee away. Immediately after this brilliant campaign, Trung Trac was proclaimed sovereign by the people, with the title Trung Vuong [Queen Trung]. She set up her capital at Me Linh, in the present province of Vinh Phuc. It was the first investiture of a royal title in the history of our people, and it happened to be conferred on a woman. Thus, after having borne the Chinese feudalists' yoke for nearly three centuries, our country, under the leadership of a woman, with a hard struggle regained its right to independence.

The reaction of the Chinese court promptly followed. A great feudal power in Asia, the China of the Hans could not allow a province on the doorstep of the empire to take back its freedom by force of arms. In the year A.D. 42, after two years of careful preparation, the Chinese emperor ordered Ma Yuan, a great strategist, to go and fight against Trung Vuong. Assisted by his best lieutenants, Ma Yuan penetrated Giao Chi territory and got as far as Lang Bac, in present-day Bac Ninh province.

Trung Vuong went with her army to encounter Ma Yuan and fought battle after battle against him. Vanquished by an army greater in number, better organized, better equipped, and commanded by a veteran warrior, the two sisters fell back to the Hat Giang [present-day Day River], where they committed suicide by drowning. It was in the year A.D. 43.

In various regions of the country, the resistance went on bitterly and fiercely. But finally the insurgent army was crushed. For a second time, the country fell under the domination of the Chinese feudalists.

Despite its unfortunate end, the insurrection of the two Trung sisters has remained a symbol of the indomitable spirit of our people. Old prints depict the two sisters seated on the backs of elephants, dressed as warriors, their heads encircled with yellow turbans. In the fervent homage rendered to their heroines, the people did not want to admit that they had been defeated by the enemy and driven to suicide. According to the *Thien nam ngu luc* (*Extracts from Tales of the South*), a literary work dating from the seventeenth century, they entered the abode of the immortals. The people's admiration and faith in them have deified them, and every year, with the return of spring, on the sixtieth day of the second moon, the people of Hanoi celebrate the anniversary

The long streams of hair (a symbol of virginity), the *ao dai*, and the sitting position typify traditional Vietnamese femininity.

(*Photo: Pham Van Mui*)

of the death of "the two ladies" in the commemorative temple of Dong Nhan, which is dedicated to them.

"THE TRANSLUCENT BEAUTY OF THE AO DAI," BY *Trong Nhan* (in *Saigon Daily News*, June, 1968)

Vietnamese women have long been admired for their graceful appearance, and their charm is enhanced by the floating beauty of their national dress, the ao dai. *It should be remembered that this lovely dress is a sign of luxury as well as femininity; made of silk or diaphanous material stretching to the ankles, worn over black or white silk trousers, the* ao dai *is not work-day wear. A peasant woman may own one* ao dai *to wear to town or on feast days, but her usual clothes—and those of the working-class urban woman, too—consist of black cotton trousers, a black or white cotton blouse and, for the outdoors, a conical hat.*

The traditional Vietnamese woman's dress, the *ao dai* is considered by Westerners to be one of the most elegant and feminine national costumes in the world. Over the last thirty years, the *ao dai* has undergone many changes. French influence has contributed to its present uncluttered, flowing charm. Unlike the tight-fitting Chinese *cheongsam,* which tends to restrict movement, the Vietnamese *ao dai,* with its close-fitting bodice, free-flowing front and back panels, and long black or white silk trousers is a delicate and airy garment. Though these long, flowing panels are something of a hazard when riding a bicycle or sitting side-saddle on a motor scooter, Vietnamese women consider that the *ao dai's* advantages far outweigh its drawbacks—especially when it comes to hiding unshapely legs, thick ankles, or knobby knees.

Almost all over the world, people are familiar with the *ao dai*. Many Vietnamese girls who travel overseas to study wear their graceful dress. Wives of Vietnamese VIP's, such as Mrs. Nguyen Van Thieu and Mrs. Nguyen Cao Ky, always draw admiring glances on official visits. Though many European and American women have tried to wear the *ao dai*, it rarely does them justice. The frail pieces of streaming material seem unbecoming to them, because, in general, they are taller and larger boned than the tiny, slender Vietnamese women.

Fashions have changed too. Some thirty years ago, the dress, though still basically resembling today's fashion, was loose-fitting and reached only below the knees. The back fell straight from the neck, while the front formed two separate pieces that tied at the waist, the left tie always being larger than the right. This left a gaping V across the chest, which was covered by a piece of cloth tied behind the neck. Some fifteen years later, the dress received several improvements. The gaping V neck was reduced to a more demure size and, the two ends, instead of being tied together, were allowed to fall freely.

And so the revolution continued. The French eliminated the knots and belts, and the bodice changed to the traditional Chinese style. This tended to represent a fusion of Oriental and Western fashion. There was a stage when the shoulders were padded, but this soon passed. At least, as far as the collar is concerned, practicality has replaced fashion. For a time, women raised their mandarin collars from two centimeters to eight, but they found that it was difficult to eat. Also, their necks were held so stiffly that it was difficult even to talk. So, for the sake of comfort, collars were reduced to three centimeters. Today, however, necklines vary according to individual tastes; round, square, or heart-shaped. The collarless line is favored at the moment. The former First Lady of South Vietnam, Madame Ngo Dinh Nhu, set a trend in necklines. She wore a plunging rounded neckline which was widely imitated.

Cannot Eat My Fill

Some modern Vietnamese women find a happy medium between traditional Vietnamese dress and Western dress, though many prefer the *ao dai.* One student pointed out: "I don't have any prejudice against western skirts and dresses, but the *ao dai* pleases me." One female civil servant said: "I wear both Western and Vietnamese. The Vietnamese dress is best in cool weather, but when it is hot, Western dress is more comfortable. Whenever I am invited to dinner, I prefer to wear Western dress, so that I can eat my fill. If I eat too much, I find that the *ao dai* becomes too tight at the waist."

Young men believe the *ao dai* is old-fashioned and representative of the days when girls and boys were not allowed to associate. The older folks vary. Some say that Western dress is "not serious enough—European clothes look provocative." Others feel that young women should dress as they please. "We cannot force them to adopt our ideas. The character of girls shows in their behavior and upbringing, not in the way they dress."

"THE IDEAL VIETNAMESE WIFE," BY *Nghiem Toan*
(in *Viet My*, December, 1966)

One of the popular subjects of Vietnamese literature centers on the notion of the ideal Vietnamese wife. In just about every case, she comes either from a wealthy family or a noble class. She is the daughter of a minister, a landlord, or a mandarin. The curious thing is that she always falls in love with a very poor but deserving young man. He is either a farmer or the son of a once prominent family who is penniless at the time she knows him. From this, one of the good qualities of the ideal Vietnamese wife has already been singled out: Deep in her heart, there is no class distinction, no prejudice. When it comes to love, she has no concern for money or class, which, considering everything else in Vietnam, is quite revolutionary.

No matter what problems she has to face, this ideal wife always proves herself to be sincere, faithful, enduring, and unselfish. "I'll stand through thick and thin by my husband and endure the coldness by myself," she will always say. The most typical of these women is Cuc Hoa, the heroine of a popular play described here by Professor Nghiem Toan.

Tong Chan, a young boy of eight, and his mother were reduced to begging after his father's death. One day, as they begged at the farm of a wealthy landlord, the daughter of the house took pity on him, gave him a bowl of rice, and asked about his misfortune. Her father discovered them talking, and since good girls were not supposed to talk to strangers, the father became angry and forced her to marry Tong Chan. She was then thirteen, five years older than he. In the tradition of good wives, she took care of the mother-in-law and worked hard to help him through school. He passed his exams and . . . received his doctorate. The king, impressed with the young scholar, wanted him to marry his daughter, but Tong

Chan refused. The princess became angry and persuaded the king to send him as ambassador to China for ten years, leaving his family behind. To be sent to China was, at the time, like being put in exile. Through several hard tests given by the Chinese king, Tong Chan proved himself to be an able and intelligent scholar. The Chinese king, holding him in high esteem, wanted him to marry his daughter, but again Tong Chan modestly refused, for he did not want to forsake his wife at home.

Seven-Year Hitch

After her husband had been away for almost seven years, without sending any news to her, his wife was pressed by her father to remarry a wealthy district chief. She refused, and both she and her mother-in-law were locked up. God came to her aid, helping her to slip away to Ba Vi Mountain, where a spirit agreed to take a message to her husband in China.

Conservative schoolgirls in Hue stroll by the gate of the old Citadel. A modern concrete bunker has been added to the top of the rampart.

(Photo Horst Fass, Associated Press)

She got an answer from her husband saying that she should be faithful and wait for him for three more years, but she was immediately caught by her father. To settle the case rapidly, he accepted the proposal of the district chief, who had come for her hand. After three years, the ceremony took place, with big feasts and hundreds of guests. At the height of the ceremony, Tong Chan came back disguising himself as a beggar to test his family. After stopping the wedding he rewarded those who were kind to him and who were not in favor of the wedding. He punished all those who took part in the wedding knowing that Cuc Hoa was already married.

One day on his hunt in the forest in search of venison to treat the queen's tuberculosis, Tong Chan came face to face with the Chinese princess who out of love had come all the way from China to look for him. The Vietnamese king agreed to her marriage to Tong Chan. Without being jealous Cuc Hoa accepted the fact gracefully and suggested that the princess be the first-rank wife, but the princess said in turn that, since she had come later, she should be of second rank.

To solve the problem, Tong Chan suggested a contest of household skills. Cuc Hoa emerged the winner and, therefore, was the first lady of the house. The three lived together happily the rest of their lives.

"SO MANY GIRLS, AND NOT ENOUGH HUSBANDS," BY *Nguyen Thuoc* (in *Vietnam Magazine*, 1969)

Vietnamese women have the reputation of being among the loveliest in Asia: Their natural charm and femininity have won the heart of many visitors. And there are so many of them: the streets of any city, from Saigon to Hue, abound in young, elfin beauties. Still, many handsome and well-bred

Vietnamese girls have great difficulties in finding the husband of their choice, anyone elegible to wed, for that matter. This shortage of Vietnamese husbands has led an increasing number of Viet namese girls to marry foreigners and settle abroad, though many would certainly prefer to remain in their native land. The obvious reason for this peculiar situation is the military draft, which keeps nearly one million young men under the flag, away from home and away from the girls.

In a popular Saigon tune, a teenage daughter wails to her mother, "I want to get married!" The reply is a sympathetic, "My dear, I am of the same mind as you!" Unhappily, this song confirms sad statistics gathered by the South Vietnamese Government. The war has upset the balance of the sexes, and many a Vietnamese girl may be doomed to spinsterhood. In Saigon alone, there are some 190,000 unmarried women—and only 75,000 bachelors. According to the Institute of Statistics, the preponderance of females is in the twenty-five

A forklift operator at an American military warehouse in Long Binh. Some nineteen thousand Vietnamese, the majority of them women, work for this huge operation.

to thirty-five-year-old age group, where there are 100 men for every 166 women. Most of the males are in the armed forces, away from home, and many have been killed in action. This tragic loss of so many young men has upset the traditional pattern of Vietnamese life. Where once men tilled the farms, most of the work is now done by women. The farms have been hit not only by the war but also by the lure of more money and the bright lights of the cities. Thousands of men have left their women to farm the land while they took off for jobs in the urban areas.

But even this movement away from the rural areas has not balanced the sex ratio in cities like Saigon. The Institute estimates that of some 110,000 commercial jobs in the capital, over 67,000 are held by women. Many factories and offices have been forced to hire women to replace their male employees called to the colors. One plant employs 500 workers, and only 40 per cent are male, with three out of four over 30 years old. Only five years ago the entire work force was male. Some factory managers don't like this change. "The output in our place" said one of them "is not as good as before, because most of these women work on a temporary basis. Our male employees are generally more stable and dedicated to their jobs, because they hope to stay with the company till retirement." But others, especially in some of the large construction firms, have expressed their satisfaction and admiration for the young girls employed in such heavy-duty work as driving tractors, trucks, and operating cranes, bull-dozers, and similar types of heavy machinery.

Another big problem that has affected matrimony is inflation. Statistics show that only 15 per cent of young men around twenty-five are getting married. Not long ago, a farming youth of eighteen was already raising a family. Nguyen Thanh Trung, twenty-eight and an engineer, explained his plight: "I expect to be in the army in a few months. If I marry now, we won't have time to set up our own home.

Besides, the expenses are considerable: 10,000 piasters (US$ 85) for a wedding gown and suit; 40,000 piasters (US$ 340) for a wedding ring; car rental and a wedding party may run as high as 50,000 piasters (US$ 420)." Trung estimated that a suitable wedding would cost him 100,000 piasters (US$ 850), and, in addition, he would need at least that much to rent and furnish a decent home. This is almost prohibitive for a young man whose salary does not exceed 15,000 piasters (US$ 125) per month.

Miss Trinh Thi Mai, twenty-three, a Saigon student, is only too acutely aware of the problem. Wryly, she quotes a Vietnamese proverb that says "Thirty-year-old men are still young, but thirty-year-old women are already getting old." This crisis has its impact on the behavior of young Vietnamese girls. According to Miss Mai: "Many schoolgirls who before were serious and dedicated are turning into hippies and get involved in all sorts of affairs with young men primarily because they don't know what the future will bring. Young men in a city like Saigon only like to "date" their girl friends but they are not interested in marriage. And when they do marry, they don't—like before—marry the demure, virgin types but a girl who already has a steady job or a good profession. It is not that these boys are fortune hunters—they are just concerned about some kind of security. I know one boy who says when he goes into the army, he wants his wife to help support the family, because he won't make enough on his soldier's pay."

One result has been that many girls have lowered their sights for eligible husbands. Today, a bride's father may well be persuaded to pay part or even all of the wedding expenses. But, even so, the big problem is—how to catch a husband and keep him. Hasty marriages, financial pressures, and unsettled social conditions have greatly increased the divorce rate. Last year, Saigon courts processed about three thousand divorce cases—and this in a country that still considers family ties sacrosanct.

LIFE

"HOW TO SHOOT AN ELEPHANT IN VIETNAM"
(*Anonymous*, 1968)

Relations between Vietnamese officials and their American counterparts are often strained by seemingly trivial incidents involving local pride and prejudices as well as cultural differences. In the story recounted below, however, the matter appears to have been handled with appropriate tact.

At approximately 1600 hours one wet day of August, Frank Wisner, the Adviser in Tuyen Duc Province, was approached in his office at the provincial headquarters by one Lt. Tao. "The provincial chief would like to see you", announced the lieutenant. "It is urgent." Wisner dropped his reading and proceeded to the office of the provincial chief, Col. Bich. Entering, he sensed trouble. A full array of senior provincial officials were gathered around the chief's desk, gazing morosely at the floor. Wisner nodded courteously and took his seat. His arrival was barely acknowledged, and seconds ticked by. Abruptly, Col. Bich raised his head and said: "We have an embarrassing incident."

The colonel coughed. No one else uttered a sound.

"I am sorry to report," he continued, "that American soldiers coming up Route 20 to Dalat murdered the elephant at the zoo. Here, you read Vietnamese," said Col. Bich, passing Wisner a rumpled scrap of onion-skin paper. "Read the report."

The report bore witness to the following incident:

> SUBJECT: Accidental Shooting of Elephant.
>
> 1. 13 Aug. 1968, at approximately 1300 hours, one of the elephants at the Pren Zoo, located Duc Truong District, was wounded.
>
> 2. Preliminary investigation revealed that U.S. personnel were involved by discharging their weapons in the area, wounding said elephant.
>
> 3. U.S. veterinarians have been dispatched to the area to administer to the supposedly critically wounded animal.
>
> 4. Further details will be forwarded as soon as available.

Wisner, making mental note of the fact that, if it is difficult to shoot an elephant in the jungle, it is considerably more difficult to shoot one in a zoo, hung his head in shame. The provincial chief then reminded Wisner of the esteem in which the elderly elephant (variously estimated at forty to fifty years of age) was held by the populace of Dalat, and that this represented yet another blow at the declining fortunes of the Pren Zoo.

"Measures, of course, must be taken," said Col. Bich.

Uttering apologies, Wisner quickly summoned his deputy, Lt. Col. Arthur Deverill, to help shoulder the blame. Col. Deverill arrived, was apprised of the facts, and offered his condolences. Col. Bich then announced the formation of an Elephant Investigation Committee, chaired by the Chief of Animal Husbandry and including the ARVN S-5 (Public Affairs Officer) and a hapless U.S. Army first lieutenant, chosen by Wisner for his owlish and lawyer-like appearance.

The Elephant Investigation Committee visited the elephant and verified that, while wounded, it remained "operational," as evidenced by droppings and the fact that it took occasional nourishment from zoo attendants. As a result, two U.S. Army veterinarians were sent by helicopter from Cam Ranh Bay to make a determination as to whether the elephant could be saved. The veterinarians soon realized that, since the elephant was lying on its wounded side, it would have to be turned over in order to permit a full examination. A call to the 362nd Signal Company in Dalat brought forth a task force, including one jeep that became stuck in the mud; one five-ton wrecker that snapped its drive-shaft attempting to extricate the jeep; and one armored personnel carrier that, after four hours, succeeded in rigging and turning the elephant.

While a crowd of Montagnard tribesmen, local children, zoo-keepers, and the zoo's remaining able-bodied elephant (a one-tusked beast expropriated from the estate of Madame Nhu) looked on, the veterinarians—whose activities had previously been confined to the treatment of dogs, pigs, and water buffaloes—proceeded to examine their patient. They climbed over the prostrate beast, attempted to probe its wounds and to insert a rectal thermometer—an operation that left them up to their elbow in it. They concluded that complications had set in and the elephant would probably die.

These findings were reported to the provincial chief through the Elephant Investigation Committee, and Col. Bich decided that the elephant would have to be dispatched. To this purpose, he named an Elephant Execution Subcommittee largely recruited from the ranks of the provincial government and included the Animal Husbandry, Montagnard, Administrative, and Agricultural services.

The subcommittee initially became mired in the paperwork that invariably accompanied all activities, no matter how trivial. Requisite documents had to be drawn up at the zoo, at the Animal Husbandry Service, and at village, district, and provincial levels. One elephant-execution detail was forced to turn back for lack of an authorizing document. A second mission was thwarted by fog. On the third attempt, the elephant was dispatched by two Vietnamese soldiers.

Meanwhile, Wisner had again been summoned to the provincial chief's office, this time to discuss disposal of the elephant's remains. Wisner recommended that the elephant meat be distributed to local Montagnard refugees, thinking it unlikely that it would tempt the palates of the more sophisticated Vietnamese. At this point, from a far corner of the room came the voice of the deputy provincial chief. "Elephant meat is very good," he said. A surprisingly large number of service chiefs and other *fonctionnaires* were found to share this opinion. When the Elephant Meat Distribution Committee was formed, it was found, in fact, to include a heavy cross-section of provincial officials and no Montagnards.

The Elephant Meat Distribution Committee now took up its responsibilities. Wisner was informed that he would get the elephant's feet. He graciously declined, only to be informed, "All Americans want elephant feet." Next, the Animal Husbandry Chief put in a bid for the elephant's entrails to feed the Pren Zoo's tiger and two leopards, who normally consume 7,000 piastres a month worth of meat. At this point, the chief of the provincial administration center, Mr. Dieu, reminded his colleagues that the trunk had not yet been spoken for. Mr. Dieu, who had more than a casual interest in certain esoteric aspects of Oriental pharmacology, remarked that elephant-trunk paté had been known to enhance male potency. The deputy provincial chief, who was scheduled to be married the following week, was all ears at this bit of news and allowed that he personally would attend to the trunk.

Finally, the moment came to carve the elephant up. Details of the actual meat distribution are somewhat obscure, but reliable sources report that a large portion of the meat did in fact reach Montagnard refugees. A fair amount also probably found its way to the larders of local officials. "Bureaucrats and soldiers poured out of their offices and billets and descended on it like mosquitoes," noted one American official in describing the arrival at provincial headquarters of a pickup truck containing portions of the elephant's remains.

An American officer claimed the feet. The deputy provincial chief was not so fortunate. His elephant trunk was last seen wiggling down a main street of Dalat on the shoulders of a minor bureaucrat. (Despite this setback, the deputy provincial chief went through with his marriage, which, reportedly, is proving successful in all respects.)

The elephant was gone, but one important matter remained . . . that of compensation for its loss. Wisner suggested that any compensation might be paid in the form of a cash donation for renovating the somewhat run-down zoo facilities. The provincial chief, concerned with the remaining elephant's emotional needs, suggested, on the other hand, that perhaps the Americans should provide a companion for him. "It must be very sad for an elephant to live alone," said Col. Bich, a bachelor, thumping his heart. "Loneliness is very sad."

The colonel considered the elephant situation all the more tragic because another Pren pachyderm had been shot several years before, apparently because an overzealous local official had conveniently stationed it along the route of a VIP hunting party. The identity of the VIP varies as to the political bias of the person telling the story, but President Thieu, Vice President Ky, and General Vinh Loc, former II Corps commanding general, are frequent candidates for the honor.

The provincial chief and his deputy finally decided to solicit the opinions of Montagnard elephant experts as to the effects of loneliness on elephants. The experts concluded that Col. Bich had overrated the emotional problems of the remaining elephant. The payment of compensation, however, remains contingent on yet another investigation, this one being pursued by American MP's at Cam Ranh.

"HOW TO BE LIKED IN VIETNAM," BY *Tran Long* (in *The Vietnam Inquirer,* June 18, 1968)

It may seem to Westerners that Vietnamese are very difficult to understand. Indeed they are, for they share neither the same values nor the same ethics as Westerners. A Vietnamese office secretary would rather quit a well-paying job than dust her desk or brew a cup of coffee for her boss. These menial chores are regarded as demeaning in Vietnam, and, after all, the secretary comes from a family where servants are paid to do these jobs. In the superficial judgment of Westerners, Vietnamese are passive, inscrutable, self-centered, and lacking the initiative usually credited for the economic success of industrialized countries. Conversely, the Vietnamese sometimes regard Westerners as ill-mannered, pushy, and always unsatisfied with their lot. Here, writer Tran Long, a well-known newspaperman in Saigon, tells us what actions, considered perfectly correct in the West, may be interpreted in Vietnam as being in bad taste or downright offensive.

Western Practices that Are Taboo in Vietnam

Westerners are prone to make comparisons, to argue the pros and cons of a decision, the weaknesses and strengths of a proposition. Neighbors experience no embarrassment in bragging about the relative merits of their cars. There is little hesitation in pointing out to one's neighbor that he should be more progressive, keep up with the times.

The botanical garden in Saigon

This practice, if carried out in Vietnam, is fraught with danger, even though no offense is intended. In the first place, such practices—argument, comparisons, boasting—are more conducive to controversy than to harmony. The Easterner prefers to avoid expressions of disagreement. Secondly, the Easterner is proud of his heritage, his culture, his way of life, and to him, international comparisons are particularly odious. He regards those who indulge in them as being arrogant and belittling. And here we have a key point: Humility is a cardinal virtue in the East. If you would be loved by Easterners, be careful not to convey a pronounced air of self-importance or arrogance.

Westerners favor the direct approach in conversation, they don't like to "beat around the bush." The Easterner indulges in more subtleties and insinuations. A direct question is considered impolite and usually is not given a straight answer. You will make more progress by avoiding a brash frontal approach in conversation. Let's look at this more closely:

A direct request to an individual is in poor taste. You will do much better by hinting around the favor desired and let the listener offer what you want. A direct request may be considered as underestimating the listener's intelligence. Take a boy-meets-girl example. A typical village Vietnamese will attempt to gain a girl's attention by singing a question:

"At this chance meeting, Plum would like to ask Peach
Whether anybody has entered the Rose Garden."

In case she does not want to start the conversation, or if she is already married, she will keep quiet. Otherwise, she may reply as follows:

"Now that Peach asks, Plum would like to answer:
The Rose Garden has an entrance, but nobody has been admitted."

Fortunately, Vietnamese do not expect foreigners to go to such an extent. But I suggest you remember that you have better odds if you avoid blunt questions and requests for favors. An experienced foreigner will not launch immediately into the business at hand. He will inquire of the children or mention some subject of mutual interest.

Americans, particularly, like to get on a first-name basis quickly. Such a practice is very effective in America: "The sweetest term in the language is the man's first name." But in Vietnam, this is interpreted frequently as undesirable familiarity. The people of the East, like many Europeans, are more reserved and prefer a warming-up or courting period. You won't lose anything by keeping things on a Mr. or Mrs. basis. Let your Vietnamese acquaintance advance to the first-name level when he is ready.

While on the subject of name; the full name of the addressee should be spelled out in correspondence. For example: Mr. Tran Van Dong, not Mr. T. V. Dong. In addition to the etiquette aspect, there is considerable possibility for error if you resort to initials.

Similar remarks apply to the question of introducing oneself to strangers. The American is not shy about introducing himself. It is different in Vietnam. A man in a respected position will be more favorably disposed if you arrange to have a mutual acquaintance effect an introduction. Frequently, the arranger will attempt to make it appear as though it is a chance meeting, but this still does not lessen the fact that self-introductions are normally not favored.

A wise man in any country refrains from giving advice too freely and too frequently. He subtly lets the idea or the benefit to be derived from the idea spring from the listener. This is particularly true in Vietnam. To overcome a natural skepticism among Vietnamese toward untried ideas, a Westerner should not push his listener into a new venture too rapidly. The Vietnamese, like the Missourian, needs a bit of showing by concrete example or demonstration.

A Westerner in Vietnam does well to shy away from discussing local politics in company. Confidentially, don't discuss local politics with a Vietnamese until you know him quite well, and only then if he is responsive. At cocktail parties, it is better to limit your conversation to pleasantries. The terms Asiatic, Annamite, native, and Indochina should be avoided today.

From early youth, the Asian is impressed with the need for self-control. Angry comments, "letting off steam," public display of affections are considered unmannerly and extremely coarse. So keep your voice down and avoid too great a display of emotions—both parties are likely to lose face.

The use of slang, and especially American slang, within a homogeneous group is quite acceptable but would lead to misinterpretation and a possible inferiority complex when there are Vietnamese present whose mastery of the foreign language is still far from good.

If you want to summon someone, please do so with a soft voice and not by waving your index finger. If you beckon someone by your finger, your gesture will be interpreted as a display of authority on your part and an indication of lack of esteem for your subordinate, whose assigned work will probably suffer by being done halfheartedly.

Whatever you do, be careful about how you use your hand in motioning someone toward you. You're sure to get a dirty look or worse if you hold your palm up and wriggle your fingers in signaling to someone. The sign is ordinarily used in Vietnam to attract the attention of dogs and children. However, if you make the same sign but hold your hand flat, palm down, nobody will take offense.

Never tap anyone on the head. Undoubtedly, it will be taken as a personal injury to the individual's human dignity and possibly as a blow to his ancestors as well. Reserve any friendly pats on the back for intimate friends who have long been exposed to foreigners. Better still, keep hands off if you don't want to offend a Vietnamese.

You may be asked to a Vietnamese friend's house. When you enter, you may show your respect to his parents and wife by a silent nod. Don't offer to shake hands with a woman. Of course, if the woman takes the initiative, then promptly and lightly shake her hand (no crushing or pumping, please).

You may notice an ancestral shrine. It is perfectly all right to look at it and even to get close to it, but under no circumstances touch any part of the shrine. One further comment—if you sit down and cross your legs, be sure neither foot is pointed toward the shrine. Similarly, a foot pointed at an individual may be offensive.

If you are invited to eat at a friend's home, let the older people start to eat before you commence. Locally, this honor is given to the seniors rather than the guests.

The common plate from which you take food to your personal plate should always have one or two things left, and under no circumstances should you take the last bit of food from it. If you clean the common plate, the hostess might feel embarrassed because she had not prepared enough food for her guest. However, once you take the food to your personal plate, it is expected that you clear your plate to show that you appreciate the hostess's good cooking and that you know what you want when you take the food.

It is bad taste to inquire about the cost or the purchase place of household articles. It is also considered bad taste in Vietnam to put one's feet on a desk, chair, or table. This is considered haughty behavior.

If you want to return a friend's courtesy by inviting him out to a restaurant, be careful to select a fairly expensive restaurant, even though the food may not be as good as at a cheaper restaurant. If you take him to a cheap restaurant, even to one serving good food, he may feel slighted.

On a chance meeting, if you are the senior, you are expected to pick up the tab. The practice of "Dutch treat," in which each one pays for himself, is not in vogue in Vietnam.

If you feel like sending a gift to a household, it is better to send something for the children rather than for the wife. An odd number of gifts is not well received. It is better to

Two musicians in blue silk robes and traditional black headgear wait in a Saigon park to play at a ceremony marking the cult of a national hero.

send two presents to a child, even though the combined cost of the two presents is less than one. This aversion to odd numbers is particularly true for wedding gifts. If you send one present to a wedding couple, it might be interpreted as a prognostic that this marriage will not last.

With Vietnamese, there is still a sharp distinction between manual labor and intellectual work. A man who styles himself an intellectual would rather do some clerical work at lower pay than work with his hands. Thus, cafeterias and other notions of self-service and do-it-yourself are still very foreign to Vietnamese life. A Vietnamese of means and dignity pays servants to work for him. He does not move a heavy object and does not help his wife with the cooking. If you like to wash your car yourself or to help around the house, it would be prudent to let your servants know that you do not mean to be a miser or to take work away from a laborer, but that you enjoy doing those things for physical exercise.

If you have picked up Vietnamese phrases from servants, it is wise to check them with a close friend before using them indiscriminately. In this connection, it would be very profitable for you to learn at least the rudiments of the Vietnamese language and a few common expressions. Vietnamese is admittedly a difficult language. However, you will receive considerable esteem and satisfaction from knowing and using the basic expressions of Vietnamese.

"VIETNAMESE NAMES MEAN A LOT," BY *George F. Schultz* (in *Viet My*, June, 1969)

The manner in which foreigners pronounce their names must be very disconcerting to the Vietnamese. If we remember that Vietnamese is a monosyllabic language, it becomes clear that the very common family name of Nguyen *is but a single syllable and that it must be pronounced as* ng-win, *never as* n-goo-yen. *It might be mentioned, too, that the Viet of Vietnam is* not *pronounced* veet, *but* vyet, *the vowel being similar to that of Russian* nyet.

The Hundred Families

It has been said that there are only ninety-nine family names in Vietnam. Why ninety-nine is a question. The legend is that the first occupants of the territory of Vietnam were divided into 100 families. This figure is, of course, too low for today, but actually there are perhaps no more than 300 names for a population of 38,000,000. This is not so surprising. After all, in China, there are only 450 family names. Of the 300 Vietnamese family names, some 200 originated in the valley and delta of the Red River, cradle of early Vietnamese culture and civilization, and today one of the world's most densely populated areas.

The family name of Nguyen is by far the most common, being used by slightly over 50 per cent of the population. There seems to be a historical reason: With the overthrow of the later Ly dynasty in 1225 by the lords of Trinh, who then established the Tran dynasty, all members of the deposed dynasty, as well as all other families using the name of Ly, were ordered to change it to Nguyen. In this manner, those in power hoped to destroy all possibility of a restoration of the Ly dynasty.

Eighty-five per cent of the population uses one of the twelve following names: Duong, Dao, Dang, Dinh, Do, Hoang or Huynh, Le, Ngo, Nguyen, Pham, Tran, Vu, or Vo.

There are a few double family names: They are joined by

a hyphen and both are capitalized: Au-Duong, Ha-Duong, Nguyen-Ha, and so on. The second of these names is often a maternal family name. The second member of a compound family name must not be confused with the intercalary name, which is properly not hyphenated.

As in the case of European family names, Vietnamese names are largely derived from common nouns—the original meaning of which has been lost or changed with the passage of time. Almost without exception, they are derived from Chinese characters. For example, the family names of Nguyen, Le, and Ngo were the names of ancient Chinese principalities. (Ngo, by extension, then came to mean China itself, but it is now so used only in a derogatory sense).

The Intercalary Name

The intercalary name or particle is a form that does not exist in the composition of Western names; it is perhaps the most confusing element of the Vietnamese name. It was necessary because through the too frequent use of the same family name it became increasingly difficult to identify an individual. In this there is some similarity with the middle name or initial used in the United States.

The most common intercalary names are those indicating sex—*Van,* male, and *Thi,* female. *Van,* meaning literature, once expressed the hope that the bearer would succeed in the literary contests and become a scholar and mandarin. *Thi* similarly expressed the hope that its bearer would be the mother of many children. These literal meanings have been lost with the passage of time.

In later life, should the individual consider that the middle name bestowed by his parents is not suitable, that is, that it does not form an ideological ensemble with his family and personal names, he may change it. For example, Huynh Van

Ngoc has no particular meaning; but when the intercalary *Nhu* (to resemble) is substituted for *Van*, we obtain "Huynh Nhu Ngoc, Huynh who resembles Jade"; in the same way, Phan Van Chau has no great beauty, but on changing the intercalary to *Minh* (clear) we have Phan Minh Chau, "Phan the Clear Gem." Nguyen Van Quang is uninspiring, but Nguyen Ngoc Quang becomes "Nguyen of Jade Resplendent." In brief, the use of the intercalary here renders the complete name rich, poetic, literary, chivalric, or patriotic. Young girls are particularly anxious to acquire a more suitable middle name.

In families of noble origin, the intercalary is almost never changed, for in so doing the identity of the family would be lost. The mandarinal Ho family of Hue retains the intercalary *Dac* in perpetuity, to distinguish it from all other (and especially lesser) families bearing the name of Ho. In the same way, a certain mandarinal Nguyen family keeps its identity by retaining *Khoa* (class, session) as intercalary.

In North and central Vietnam, the intercalary name is sometimes omitted. The complete name then consists of family name plus personal name: Pham Quynh, Le Xuan, Nguyen Binh, Pham Bich, and so on.

The intercalary particle is properly not capitalized, but it has succumbed to foreign influence and is now sometimes written that way.

The Personal Name

The third component of the complete name is the personal name, corresponding somewhat to our Christian, or given, name. Peasant families and the illiterate do not attach much importance to the choice of given names. On the other hand, in educated families, they are always the object of severe and judicious selection and are chosen to form an ideological ensemble with the family and intercalary names, and sometimes with the personal names of other members of the family.

In general, feminine personal names are taken from flowers, trees, birds, the seasons, or precious objects. Masculine names are usually taken from abstract values; however, there is no fine line, and many names are applicable to either sex. The only restriction on the choice of personal name is that the name of the father, grandfather, or other near relative must not be used.

Today, a person is referred to under almost all circumstances by his personal name, even with a title: Ong Hoa, Mr. Hoa; Ba Kim, Mrs. Kim; Co Thu, Miss Thu. If there is any confusion, the full name may be used. For obvious reasons, the family name is seldom used alone. When Vietnamese names are arranged alphabetically it is often in reference to the personal rather than the family name, although the Saigon telephone directory uses the latter.

In North Vietnam, the first-born child is often called Ca (eldest), the second, Hai (two), the third, Ba (three), the fourth, Tu (four), the fifth, Nam (five), and so on, without regard to sex; in South Vietnam, however, the first-born is called, Hai (two), the second, Ba (three), the third, Tu, and so on.

The use of numerals is resorted to for several reasons: first, for convenience: Vietnamese families are generally large, and simple numeration provides a ready means of identity; secondly, in superstitious families, one avoids pronouncing the child's correct name, in order to confuse the evil genie who are ever seeking to harm young and defenseless children. Since the eldest is always the first target of these spirits, the latter are thrown off the track by omitting any reference to the first-born as Number One, he or she being called Hai, Number Two, instead, especially in the South.

Poetic Names for Girls

Many Vietnamese women are very fond of a compound personal name or couplet, although it is rarely found in the case of men. The idea is purely one of embellishment, in an effort to create a pleasant ideological combination.

Some examples:

Xuan Hoa	Spring Flower
Thanh Thuy	Clear Water
Kim Son	Golden Mountain
Dieu Hoi	Fragrant Odor
Tuyet Mai	Snow-White Apricot Blossom

These couplets often give rise to a special situation within a given family. For example, Mr. Dao Dang Vy has three daughters, to whom he gave compound personal names, as follows: The first part of each name, Giao, recalls one of the earliest names applied to the delta of North Vietnam; the second is a common personal name. Thus, we obtain:

Dao Giao Thuy	Giao of the Propitious Augury
Dao Giao Chau	Giao the Pearl
Dao Giao Tien	Giao the Fairy

STUDENTS

"WHEN SONS OF WORKERS AND PEASANTS ENTER THE UNIVERSITY," BY *Phuong Vy*
(in *Vietnam Advances,* March, 1969)

The mandarinate system of ancient Vietnam postulated an ideal ruling elite, drawn from an educated minority, who advanced according to ability not social class. In practice, however, only the sons of wealthy families could afford the leisure and instruction necessary to pass the arduous examinations—although there were, of course, notable exceptions. In modern times, higher education has remained the province of the rich and the middle classes, although education is much prized and sought after by all. The Democratic Republic of Vietnam has provided opportunities for workers' children to get an education, in an educational system geared to combine "work and study." Yet, prejudices remain, and in the following article, students from the Complementary School for Workers and Peasants describe their difficulties in entering the University of Hanoi.

When I asked him about his childhood, Ho Van Ba's eyes clouded, and almost unconsciously he frowned, as if for a moment he lived again through those difficult times. His parents were poor boatmen of Binh Dinh [South Vietnam]. His father's small boat went from one port to another along the coast of South Vietnam, carrying tiny quantities of freight. Little Ba was in the third form when lack of means forced his parents to withdraw him from primary school and have him go into the service of a man practicing traditional Eastern medicine.

When the August, 1945, revolution broke out, he was eighteen years old and knew a few Chinese characters. The revolutionary authorities sent Ba to school for two years before entrusting him with a job in the propaganda service. After the 1954 armistice and his regroupment to the North, Ba went to work in the Ministry of Communications and Water Conservation.

His friend Vo Viet Dong is a bit younger and had received a more regular education. In his village in Nghe An province, he had gone to school as far as the seventh form * during the resistance.

"I wanted to enlist," he said, "but I was a bit short of height."

He smiled, a bit embarrassed. Although they are third-year students at the university, they have still kept their peasant outlook and are a little clumsy, but they have also retained their simple and direct manners. Dong is short of stature. In centimeters, that is beyond question . . . but morally! He worked in a shock brigade that built the road leading to Dien Bien Phu under the constant threat of napalm bombs. Among other assignments, he got a special job: to unprime the delayed-action bombs. He was lucky to find himself alive when the armistice finally came. He then stayed on in the northwest mountains to repair roads, until the day when he was allowed to resume his studies.

Thus, Ba and Dong attended together the Complementary

* Junior Secondary school.

School for Workers and Peasants, which was founded after the armistice. The 400 students of this first promotion had to work doubly hard, to become the new forces at the university.

After two years' work without a break, Ba and Dong went to the university. It was in 1956, at the moment when the *Nhan Van—Giai Pham* group and the student magazine *Dat moi*, availing themselves of the events in Hungary and of the mistakes committed during land reform, waged an active campaign against the popular democratic regime. These papers had an effect upon only a very limited public of intellectuals, bourgeois, and petty bourgeois in the capital but had found some supporters at the university. They incited the students to prove their "fearlessness" by attacking the Party, the regime, and the university. "This regime is a Party regime, it suppresses personality. . . . The level of the curriculum is too low. . . . It is leveling at the lowest plane. Down with forced discipline!" Students of worker and peasant extraction were the chief objects of attack, under the pretext that they brought down the academic level of the university.

Recalling those painful days, Ba shook his head:

"Hardly had we crossed the door of the school in our blue or *cu nau,** suits when these people pointed at us, whispering. Some went so far as to provoke us openly. Sitting near us, they said loudly enough for us to hear them: 'What do they come here for, these ignoramuses?' Obviously, these insolent fellows had graduated from a French *lycée*. Some went so far as to say: 'Let me be appointed assistant lecturer to smarten up these blockheads. After that we can study with them.'

"But we reacted. The bad elements were, after all, a minority. The Party and the labor youth organization guided our action."

Soon after, the fire-eaters of the *Dat moi* magazine could no longer think aloud without finding opposition. One day, a movement was launched in the whole university. During a

* Brown vegetable dye used by peasants in North Vietnam.

meeting in the big assembly hall, students coming from the Complementary School for Workers and Peasants talked about their earlier life. Xuan, a former student of a French *lycée* in Hanoi, told me about this meeting:

"A student took the floor. He wore a very simple blue suit, like all the cadres of the resistance. He spoke calmly, occasionally with a touch of emotion, a suddenly graver voice. But he had no need of eloquence. The subject was important enough and new enough to captivate the audience. What did he say? He spoke only of his life. And he added: 'We were like that, thousands of us, whose families had not enough rice to eat nor a piece of low-quality fabric to make a suit. We went barefoot. Never could we have hoped to receive even secondary education. Now, through sheer hard work, here we are at the university. We know that our regime will bring us happiness. There are those who clamor that there is no freedom here. But tell me, what sort of freedom are they speaking of? They say they have lost a lot, but can they tell us precisely what they have lost?' On hearing that, all those playboys who had been the loudest to complain were as dumb as fish. If they had not yet changed their minds, at least they had begun to think."

I asked Xuan what he thought of the cultural level of the students coming from the Complementary School for Workers and Peasants. "Our comrades had shortcomings in their training," he said. "It's understandable. Whose fault was it? Was it not because of the old regime of colonial obscurantism that had weighed on our country for eighty years? Nobody had the right to laugh at them. Besides, their presence here has not in the least affected the level of the lectures. They have been able to overcome their shortcomings. They have shown they could do it. Their presence here was necessary if we really wanted to change the atmosphere of the university."

"We had made enormous efforts," Ba added. "Nevertheless, in the first year, many of us were not able to follow the lectures, and I was one of them. So was Dong. We were most worried about the end-of-year exams. At night, while poring over my books, I asked myself: Should I go back to the Complementary School or do another first year? But then I remembered the encouragement of the Party committee at the university and of the headmaster of my former school: 'The people have placed their trust in you; do not let them down,' and I plunged again into my books. I went and asked for supplementary explanations from all those who could help me."

It was Xuan who told me about the results of all these obscure efforts, since Ba and Dong would be a little embarrassed to speak about them. By the end of the second year, most of the former students of the Complementary School for Workers and Peasants no longer had supplementary exams to take. They all got the "pass" marks at the regular session of exams, and many of them did much better.

The achievements of one of them, Pham Van Hap, were even made public in the five faculties. This honor was awarded only to two students. Pham Van Hap, who had managed with difficulty to follow the lectures during the first year, now got "A" marks in most subjects. And this did not prevent him from being quite active in the local section of the Labor Youth Union, of which he was the secretary.

After dinner, I paid my last visit to the boarders of the Polytechnical Institute. We came back to our subject. At present, there is no discrimination among students because of their origin.

And everybody has set to work with the same high spirits. While carrying on their studies, the students took up pick-and-shovel work to enlarge their school. They devoted nearly two months to manual work at the site of the Bac Hung Hai irrigation project in the fall of last year. The spirit of the working class has caught the university. The former students of the Complementary School for Workers and Peasants are the yeast that raises the dough.

Through the door of the room, I saw the new playground which was entirely built by the students during the last summer holidays.

Night fell. On both sides of the playground, the buildings of the old Indochinese University gradually became two big dark masses. Drowned now in the midst of scores of one-story houses which have cropped up around them these last three years, they have lost a bit of their lordly air.

We were saying goodbye. A student saw me to the large walk. "We have macadmised the walks of the school ourselves," he said. "Three years ago, someone would have said: 'Why should we? It's not our business!' Our university has completely changed. We no longer work just for a career; we prepare ourselves for the building of a socialist country."

In the South, too, university life has changed: Here, students lead a noisy street demonstration against the government.

Vietnam is plagued by a shortage of skilled workers because the system of education places too much emphasis on abstract studies. At a trade school in Saigon, apprentices learn to make sand molds for casting iron. (*AID-Saigon*)

"STUDENTS AND GIRLS OF VIETNAM SEEN THROUGH POPULAR SONGS," BY *Le Hung Chuong* (in *Asia*, September 6, 1952)

Vietnam espoused the Confucian and Chinese mandarinal system during the first millennium A.D., *while Vietnam was a vassal of China. Ostensibly, all authority emanated from the emperor, who held the "mandate of heaven." In practice, however, the bureaucracy, or mandarinate, held real power. Membership in the mandarinate, with its promises of prestige and financial rewards, was the goal for the educated classes. The student was an honored member of society, for only he could enter the mandarinate, through a system of national examinations based on Confucian thought, history, poetry, and ethics. This article describes the life of students studying for examination, as well as the girls they left behind. A student represented the prize matrimonial catch, since he was a potential member of the ruling elite.*

Students in every country are held in high esteem by the masses, because they represent the elite who will contribute greatly to the progress of society and the glory of the nation. Our traditional popular songs show that in Vietnam they received even more consideration in old times than they do today.

It is not very long since Vietnamese society was divided into four classes: The lettered class was the first, then came farmers, artisans, and tradesmen, in that order. Like the Chinese, our people loved and respected learned men. Students who succeeded in their examinations were received by the emperor and given titles: Trang Nguyen, Tham Hoa, Bang Nhan, and so on, according to the honors they had obtained. Then they were appointed mandarins and given posts at court. Students were always greatly respected in their own villages, where they received the honors due to men of high degree.

Vietnam is, of course, an agricultural society. Nearly 90 per cent of the population lives by agriculture and forms a proletarian class that, in the old days, used to be under the authority of the lettered class. It was thus that the peasants gradually became jealous and resentful at the idea that they, who represented the most important factor in society (since they provided its food) should be classed after the learned men, who produced nothing. They noticed, too, that the students who were admitted at the examinations, then appointed mandarins, and who led such a pleasant life, were mostly of their own class. They had needed no great effort to arrive at this result and had escaped with comparative ease from the hard lot of the peasants who are continually at the mercy of the sun, rain, and, above all, of destitution. It was then that a great movement of emulation grew up. From the cities to the countryside, from the capital to the farthest corners of the land, the voice of the students was heard, speaking in the name of the people: *Chang tham ruong ca, ao lien,/ Tham ve cai but cai nghien anh do!* (I do not ask for fertile rice fields or lakes full of fishes, I only ask for the writing boards and the brushes of the student.)

The country girls sang these songs for they considered the students as possible husbands who would insure their futures. Compared with the rough laborers, a student seemed ideal to them. He behaved like a gentleman; he was pleasant-mannered and full of wisdom and spoke of poetry and philosophy. Once he was received at the triennial competitions and appointed mandarin, his wife would be an honored lady. So the young girls dreamed of a fiancé who would pass this examination and return with trunks-full of gifts from the emperor, like a general returning victoriously from battle. They dreamed of the moment when: *Vong anh di truoc, vong nang theo sau* (The husband's litter goes ahead and that of the wife follows), and when the successful student enters the village in triumphant procession, followed by the emperor's soldiers.

According to an old custom of our country, only high court dignitaries had a right to litters sheltered by parasols, the number of which varied according to their rank. The students who succeeded in their examinations were received by the emperor at a special audience, then there was a banquet, during which the sovereign gave each of them a gift of a costume, a horse, or a litter, according to the place they had obtained in the competitions. The return to their village was the happiest day of their lives, since the whole population used to assemble to greet the new laureate, who would arrive majestically, on horseback, in his splendid costume. There were drums, torchlights, cheering . . . And the charming fiancée, hidden in the crowd, watched her future husband admiringly. A new horizon opened before her and she sang of/*Chong toi coi ngua vinh quy,/Hai ben co linh hau di dep duong* (My husband riding majestically into the village, soldiers and officers keeping order beside him).

Meanwhile, it was necessary to work hard in order to attain this great moment. Study began in childhood, and tasks were shared between girls and boys: *Gai thi giu viec trong nha/Khi vao canh cui khi ra theu thua/Trai thi doc sach ngam tho/Dui mai kinh su de cho kip khoa* (The girls keep house, sew and weave; the boys study, compose poems, and prepare for their examinations).

This sharing-out of work allowed the student to concentrate entirely on study and the family, with the vision of this triumphant return always before its eyes, would put all its hope in him. Everything depended on the way he worked—a glorious future, a high post at court, and the lovely fiancée who would wait for him, and who would often tell him: *Doi ben bac me cung gia,/Lay anh hay chu de ma cay trong* (Our parents on both sides are old; they count on you, since you are educated, to help them for the rest of their lives).

In the old days, most of our students used to marry very young, but they continued nevertheless with their studies, leaving their wives to look after the house. This was the tradition, and Vietnamese women carried out their duties willingly, since they had learned since childhood that it was their place to do the housework and that of the boys to "read and learn." Since they were constantly dreaming of the "glorious return" of their husbands, they were careful to see that they had no cares except their work: *Xin chang kinh su hoc kanh,/De em cay cay, cui canh kip nguoi./Mai sau xiem ao thanh thoi,/On gioi, loc nuoc doi doi hien vinh* (Let me labor and do the housework while you study. Later, when you have passed your examinations and been made a mandarin, we shall be happy all our lives).

And they would plan their daily routine, as follows: *Canh mot don cua, don nha;/Canh hai det cui, canh ba di nam./ Canh tu buoc sang canh nam,/Trinh anh day hoc cho nam lam chi* (At the first night watch, I tidy the house. At the second, I weave. I go to bed at the third. At the coming of the fifth, I will wake you so that you may study your lessons).

Most good housewives led this sort of life in Vietnam. During the day, they were out in the fields. When night fell, they stayed up late and did the housework for which they had not found time during the day. No one was surprised to see: *Chang ngoi doc sach,/Em ngoi quay to* (The husband reading, the wife weaving).

And at the fifth watch of the night, as soon as the cock had crowed, she would be up and preparing the days' work, without forgetting to wake her husband. "We shall rest later; now is the time for work," she would often say: *Nua mai chua mo khoa thi/Bang vang choi loi kia de ten anh./Bo cang cha me sam sanh./Sam nghien, sam but cho anh hoc hanh* (Later, there will be the competitions. Your name will be written on the shining board lacquered in red and gold. Then your parents will be rewarded for all they have done to make your studies possible).

The spirit of sacrifice was highly developed among the girls of Vietnam. Once they were married, they forgot themselves completely and worked incessantly for their families-in-law. A student was often obliged to leave his parents and wife in order to continue his studies in the town. Then his wife would take her place in the home and become its chief support, and the mere thought of her husband returning in a litter or on a fine horse was enough to console her.

The following verses tell of a separation: The husband sets off with his trunks entirely filled with books, while his wife accompanies him to the outskirts of the village and gives him good advice: *Anh di em o tai nha,/Hai vai ganh vac me gia con tho,/Lam than bao quan nang mua/Anh di anh lieu ganh dua voi doi* (You go, but I remain. I will watch over our old mother and our little child. I do not fear work. As for you, work well so that you may succeed in life).

The student would be constantly encouraged by her care and advice. In the town, he would avoid the gaming quarters and settle in some outlying road where he could be sure of peace and quiet. Sometimes his wife would come to visit him, or more exactly, to bring him food: *Mua he cho chi mua dong,/ Mua nao thuc ay cho chong ra di* (From Summer to Winter, during the four seasons of the year, at each season I prepare for you all that you need).

The following verses show her on the mandarin's road, wondering where her husband lives: *Het gao, thiep lai ganh di,/ Hoi tham chang hoc o thi noi nao,/Hoi tham den ngo thi vao;/Tay dat ganh xuong, mieng chao "Thua anh!"* (When you lack rice, I bring it to you. I inquire where you live. I lay down baskets of rice at your door, and greet you: "My darling!").

Who could fail to be moved by such affection? These verses are extremely simple and express a tender love, combined with the respect due to a husband and with unquenchable hope. It has sometimes happened that our "student-husband" did not want to see the wife who had taken so much trouble for him. He would forbid her to bring the rice herself, since the way was long and hot. Then she would smile and reply: *Em la con gai Phung-Thien,/Ban rau, mua but, mua nghien cho chong./Mot mai chong chiem bang rong/Bo cong bon tuoi vun trong cho rau* (I am a girl from the region of Phung Thien. I go to market and sell vegetables to buy brushes and tablets for my husband. Later, my husband will pass his examinations, so it is well worth growing vegetables now.).

The courageous wife would have one aim only: her husband's success; and he himself could not but recognize all she did for him: *Qua cau nho, cai vo van van./Nay anh hoc gan, mai anh hoc xa . . ./Tien bac thi cua me cha,/Cai nghien cai but thuc la cua Em!* (The areca nut is small, its shell is slightly mottled. Today I will stay with you, and tomorrow I shall be gone. The rice and money I need belong to my old parents. But my brush and tablet truly belong to you).

There were certain people, however, who detested the students. These were usually ignorant peasants who could not bear "that sort of individual" who spent his time writing poems and reading books, who could not labor in the rice fields, and, worse still, "did not know how to tie a cock's claws tightly": *Dai lung ton vai, an no lai nam!* (His back is long and needs much cloth).* He does nothing but fill his stomach and lie all day on his bed, and this is why his back is so long.

But to these criticisms, the young girl would reply as follows: "The student is like the tiger or the panther that live hidden in the forest. But when he has passed his examinations, he is like the terrible dragon that uncurls itself in the sky. Poor soul! Was so much cloth needed for his back in those days? Now he wears satin and cloth offered by the emperor."

That is the reason why all Vietnamese girls dreamed of marrying a student.

And when they used to say: *Lay chong cho dang tam chong,/Bo cong trang diem ma hong rang den!* (I can only marry a man worthy to be my husband, worthy of my rosy cheeks and *black teeth* †) . . . they were thinking of their favorite student.

* It takes a lot of material to make a robe for him.

† See Dr. Pierre Huard, *Asia,* Nos. 2 and 4, *Teeth-Blackening in East Asia and in Indochina.*

PART TWO

A Turbulent History

The Southern mountains and rivers belong
to the Viet people,
It was so clearly written in the Celestial Book.
Those who dare to attack our territory,
Will be immediately and pitilessly annihilated.

Marshal Ly Thuong Kiet
The Tông (Song) vanquisher
(XI th Century)

李常傑
Lý Thường Kiệt

The pledge of an eleventh-century national hero as it appears in a contemporary North Vietnamese magazine.

VIETNAM BEFORE THE TWENTIETH CENTURY

"ORIGIN AND MEANING OF THE NAME VIETNAM," BY *Thai Van Kiem*

On June 16, 1958, Mr. Thai Van Kiem, assistant director of the Cultural Affairs Section of the Education Department (Republic of Vietnam), gave a talk on the origin of the name Vietnam *in fact and folklore. The following is the translation of part of his talk. Mr. Kiem is now serving with the Foreign Service of the Republic of Vietnam.*

How and when did this land come to be called Vietnam?

The sound "Viet" is the pronounciation of a Chinese character meaning "far off," "beyond," or "to cross over, to go beyond." In the Chinese mind, the word conveyed the idea of a distant land, far away from China proper, which seeks freedom and expansion. These connotations will ever remain the characteristics of the Vietnamese race.

The word Viet was used for the first time in the eleventh century B.C., during the Chu dynasty (1050–249 B.C.), to designate territories located southeast of China and on the Pacific border. A descendent of Emperor Vu was crowned king of all of these remote countries—the Viet countries—around 1042 B.C.

In the years 496–465 B.C. the kingdom was ruled by Lac Long, also called Cau Tien, of the Long (dragon) family. War had just swept over the country, and now the aftermath of a serious defeat jeopardized the existence of the reduced kingdom. Cau Tien was fiercely determined to take revenge and regain his territories. It was not possible to consider resuming the battle with arms. And so a trick would be used. Advised by Pham Lai, King Cau Tien presented the conquerer, King Ngo Phu Sai, with a present which was not unusual then. He offered him Tay Thi, who was recorded by history as the most beautiful woman of these ancient times. She seduced the conquerer into discharging his wisest advisors, and his power declined. Cau Tien was thus able to annex Ngo Phu Sai's territories. Later, early in the fifth century B.C., he extended his power over Bach Viet [the hundred remote areas] along the coast, which included present North Vietnam. The powerful king then dispatched one of his sons and a strong fleet to the mouth of the Red River. They established a principality named Viet Chuong. A brass junk was sunk in the sea to mark its territorial limits.

When the limits of the new principality had been defined, it was renamed Van Lang, meaning "land of learned people." Its totems were a horse (*giao* or *keo*) and the willow (*duong lieu*). For several centuries, the Lac Viet were to worship these two signs.

In brief, the first kingdom of the Viet was founded on the southern coast of China in 1042 B.C., some 3,000 years ago, and the first Viet Chuong or Lac Viet kingdom in North Vietnam 2,400 years ago, at the beginning of the fifth century B.C. Since then, the name has been changed several times, depending on historical events. It was, successively:

Van Lang	Under the Hung or Lac dynasty (257 B.C.)
An Lac	Under the Thuc dynasty (257–207 B.C.)
Nam Viet	Under the Trieu dynasty (207–11 B.C.)
Giao Chi	Under the Han dynasty (first part) (111 B.C.–A.D. 203)
Giao Chau	Under the Han dynasty (second part) (A.D. 203–544)
Van Xuan	Under the Ly dynasty (A.D. 544–603)
An Nam	Under the Duong dynasty (A.D. 603–939)
Dai Co Viet	Under the Dinh dynasty (968–1054)
Dai Viet	Under the Ly and Tran dyasties (1054–1400)
Dai Ngu	Under the Ho dynasty (1400–1407)
Dai Viet	Under the Le and Nguyen dynasties (1427–1802)
Vietnam	Name given by King Gia Long in 1802
Dai Viet	Name given by King Minh Mang in 1832
Vietnam	Name resumed in April, 1945, by the first national government of Vietnam.

The ethnic origin of the present Vietnamese people is different from that of the Han people along the Yellow River. These are Chinese, strictly speaking. Before they expanded southward, the Viet people in the delta of North Vietnam included people of Indonesian origin and those from the valley of the Yang Tse Kiang (Blue River) in Mongolia.

These immigrants, who settled on the coast, gradually proceeded into the inner land and pushed the natives, including the Muong of Hoa-Binh and Thanh-Hoa, back towards the highlands. The phonetics and syntaxes of the dialects of these nations enabled them to be considered as part of the Vietnamese group.

Gradually the Vietnamese progressed southward, but still along the coast. For the first time, after fifteen centuries of settlement in North Vietnam, they came to Annam in 1069, Hue in 1306, Quang Ngai in 1402, Binh Dinh in 1470, Phu Yen in 1611, Nha Trang in 1653, Saigon in 1674, Phan Thiet in 1697, and Ha Tien in 1714.

"THE DIEN HONG CONFERENCE," BY *Do Van Minh*
(in *Viet Nam, Where East and West Meet*,
Edizioni Quattro Venti, Rome, 1968)

For the first thousand years A.D., *China ruled Vietnam as a province. Chinese culture and political organization dominated traditional Vietnam, geographically centered around the Red River Delta. In* A.D. 939, *Vietnam gained independence, although retaining a relationship of nominal vasselage to her large and powerful northern neighbor. The period of Vietnamese territorial expantion southward, into what is now central and South Vietnam, began. Relations with China did not always remain peaceable, however. The Dien Hong conference concerns one such conflict with China, this time in the thirteenth century.*

Shall We Yield to the Enemy?

It was in the year 1283. Vietnam was ruled by King Tran Nhon Ton, whose army was under the command of General Tran Quoc Tuan. At that time, the Mongols governed China; having interrupted their march to the West after the death of Genghis Khan, they sought an extension of their conquests by pushing south. To the Mongols, Vietnam appeared to be a very tempting bait: She was linked to colossal China along her northern border, as a province of the motherland, while, on the other hand, she constituted a gateway to Southeast Asia.

The Mongols requested passage through Vietnam in order to punish Champa—then a state in what is now central-south Vietnam—whom they condemned for having failed to pay tribute. Upon the refusal of their demands, they immediately crossed the frontier in full force. After many battles, they occupied the capital of Vietnam, in addition to many other towns.

One night, King Tran Nhan Ton called for General Tran Quoc Tuan and addressed him thus: "Dear General, I know that all your life you have helped me to vanquish the enemy in the course of many battles. You have never fought a battle without being victorious, but this time I am not sure that we can successfully resist. Since my only desire is to keep peace for my subjects, it might be best to yield to the enemy's demands."

The King's Dilemma

General Quoc Tuan replied: "I know that throughout my life, Your Majesty, you have constantly praised and assisted me. My duty is to pay implicit obedience to your Majesty. I would rather die on the field of battle in defense of our honor than suffer defeat. It is true that our enemies are numerous, but since we all are firmly determined to resist, I do not doubt that we shall soon repulse the foe."

The king hesitated: "I am still worried that our people will resent this war very much."

The general then suggested: "Let us call together the elders of all classes; let them decide whether to fight or to yield."

For the first time in the history of Vietnam, a king left to his people the decision of their fate. (It is worthwhile noting that this happened in the thirteenth century.)

Within three days, the representatives of the people from every part of the country arrived at the provisional capital to attend the conference. From the hinterland came young warriors wearing swords. There were old men who walked slowly, leaning on their staffs. Those who came from very far carried bundles of dried rice on their shoulders. In spite of old age and the obstacles posed by rivers and hills on the way, they quickened their steps.

Much moved, the king told his subjects the purpose of the conference and then concluded: "Dear People, I think I need not tell you that our country is in danger. Its solution depends upon every single Vietnamese. However, I must not hide the fact that the Mongols are already in our land, and our beloved capital is already in their hands. Under these sad circumstances in our history, I am thinking, above all, of the interests of my people. Now, you are all free to declare whether we should yield or fight."

Fight! Fight!

One old man rose and said: "Your Majesty, we feel ashamed for not having paid our debt to our country; yet, day and night, we wish to sacrifice ourselves. We would die so that our race may live."

Some one interrupted him: "Then, should we yield or fight?"

"Fight! fight!" all shouted together.

The king called the conference to a close with these words: "It is the people's desire to fight. Sooner or later, victory will be ours."

Then, to comply with the decision reached at Dien Hong, every Vietnamese fighter had his hand inscribed with two words: *Sat Dat* [Kill the Mongols]. Overcoming successive difficulties at the cost of tears and blood, the Viets at last defeated the invading armies. They were able to erase the words "Kill the Mongols," but they would never forget the historic conference of Dien Hong.

"HOW VIETNAM CONTAINED CHINA," BY *Tran Van Dinh* (in *The Washingtonian*, October, 1968)

Those who are familiar with the Asian scene know that the 3,000-year history of the Vietnamese has been characterized by their persistent and successful resistance against the domination of their colossal northern neighbor. What few people realize is that the Vietnamese policy of containment of China was not always carried out by generals and soldiers, but often by scholars and intellectuals with their wit and poetry. The Vietnamese had a keen awareness of Chinese power, and took up arms only as a last resort. Their desire to live in peace with Peking was also motivated by their wish to be left alone to pursue their Nam Tien, *or March to the South, which took them more than 800 years as they moved from the overpopulated delta of the Red River in North Vietnam to the rich Ca Mau plains in the extreme South.*

After the tenth century, although Vietnam was no longer a province of China, she always recognized the nominal suzerainty of Peking. The Vietnamese emperors in return asked that their position and the integrity of their territory be respected and guaranteed by the Chinese rulers. Following each and every one of their successful military operations against the Chinese invaders, the Vietnamese court would sue for peace. To save face for the Chinese, the Vietnamese emperors went so far as to blame (officially, of course) the "irresponsible behavior" of some Vietnamese military leaders

Tran Hung Dao, a thirteenth-century marshal, with 200,000 warriors, defeated an army of 500,000 Mongol invaders. His cult remains as alive in Saigon as it does in Hanoi—a symbol of the national will to resist foreign invaders.

for the cause of Vietnamese victories. The Vietnamese emperors would then dispatch an embassy to Peking to present their case and reaffirm their peaceful intentions.

These embassies were not permanent institutions as they exist today. They were just official visits made on special occasions, such as the change of dynasties in China or in Vietnam, or in the aftermath of an armed conflict between the two countries. The Vietnamese used these diplomatic exchanges to keep informed of the situation in China and to learn of their progress in medicine, astronomy, geomancy, and literature.

For their part, the Chinese emperors demanded to see the representatives of the Vietnamese people in person before they would confer title of Emperor on the Vietnamese monarch. For the Son of Heaven, seated on his dragon throne in the Forbidden City in Peking, at the center of the universe, there were only two kinds of people on earth: the civilized, that is the Chinese (and those who possessed a deep understanding of the thoughts of Confucius), and the barbarians, who needed to be converted to Chinese civilization by placing themselves under the cultural tutelage of the Middle Empire, as China called itself. Knowing that the Chinese held scholars, philosophers, and poets in high esteem, the Vietnamese envoys to Peking were top poets and writers—especially those endowed with wit, a gift for quick repartee, and the ability to answer quickly a poetical challenge thrown at them by their Chinese counterparts. Above all, they had to know how to compose almost instantaneously a sentence, parallel and antagonistic at the same time in words and in meaning, to the one directed at them by their Chinese opponents. Once the Peking court was satisfied with the high cultural development of the small southern neighbor, then other matters of importance could be discussed, such as the amount and the

Le Loi, honored as the architect of Vietnam's national unity, founded the Le Dynasty in 1428, after a ten-year war of liberation against the Chinese. The Le Dynasty ruled until 1788, when the Chinese again invaded Vietnam.

nature of the tribute the Vietnamese had to pay, usually every two years. The tribute normally consisted of elephant tusks, rhinoceros horns, and silk. Gold and silver objects were not on the compulsory list.

Despite the fact that for 2000 years Vietnam has been called *Van Hien Chi Bang* (The Cultured State) by the Chinese, the Chinese usually sent their own ambassadors to check on the degree of culture and civilization of the Vietnamese, not only of the elite but also of the man in the street. Sometimes the Chinese, well advanced in astronomy and geomancy, detected in their reading of the constellations certain auspicious stars shining in the southern sky, indicating the presence in Vietnam of great men and brave warriors. It was important for the Chinese military planners to confirm this information on the spot before they made the next move. To impress the Chinese envoys (or, to put it bluntly, to fool them), the Vietnamese emperors would order poets and writers to disguise themselves as boatmen, casual peasants, or even beggars to greet the plenipotentiaries from the Son of Heaven and to engage them in literary jousts. Relying only on the readings of the stars (a rather imprecise although generally reliable science) and having no resident diplomats and political officers, it was very difficult, if not impossible, for the Chinese visitors to know the difference between the Vietnamese literati and the Vietnamese masses. Naturally, after a series of encounters with highly educated Vietnamese "common men," the Chinese envoys would bring back favorable reports on the "high state of culture in the land of the south."

Mystics, Poetry, Wit

Vietnamese history and folklore are filled with anecdotes on the Chinese-Vietnamese diplomatic relations. One of the hero-diplomats who forced the respect of the Chinese for a considerable period of time was Mac Dinh Chi. At a young age, he received his doctorate of letters, at the imperial triennial examinations held under Emperor Tran Anh Ton in 1304. His literary talents, however, were not at first fully appreciated by the Vietnamese emperor, as he was rather short and ugly. But his subsequent performances in the literary field convinced the monarch that he was the country's top

The Khai Dinh tombs outside Hue still display some of the imperial grandeur of this ancient city. (*Photo: JUSPAO-Saigon*)

scholar and was therefore the natural choice to lead Vietnamese diplomatic missions to China. Soon, the choice proved the happiest one. Mac Dinh Chi enjoyed an unparalleled prestige at the Chinese court, which conferred upon him the unprecedented title of *Luong Quoc Trang Nguyen* (The First Doctor for the Two Lands), putting him *de facto* at the head of the Chinese intellectual community as well. The Chinese, it seems, attached less importance to physical appearances than the Vietnamese.

In one of his missions to Peking, the Imperial Court was in the first phase of a period of national mourning: The emperor's only daughter had just passed away. But our ambassador was not informed of this important event and, as requested by the Book of Imperial Etiquette, he went to the imperial palace to present his credentials. There he was commanded by the Chinese emperor to declaim a eulogy to the late princess on behalf of the entire diplomatic corps "representing all countries from all corners of the world and from the four seas." The Chinese chief of protocol handed him the text of the eulogy. To his surprise, he saw nothing in it but four characters: *Nhat*, meaning "one," or "unique." There was no time for panic, argument, or refusal. The occasion was solemn, the destiny and the prestige of Vietnam were at stake. If our ambassador failed to understand the riddle, he would anger the Son of Heaven and Vietnam would be condemned to untold sufferings. Calmly, Ambassador Mac Dinh Chi raised the red paper decorated with golden figures of the phoenix (in China, the symbol for woman) above his head, and in a grave voice filled with sorrow, he read:

> Oh! Beautiful Princess!
> You were indeed not long ago
> A cloud floating in the blue sky,
> A flake of snow exposed to the blazing sun,
> A blossomed bough in the Imperial Garden,
> A moon reflecting in the Fairy Lake.
> Alas! The cloud is dispersed,
> The snow is melted,
> The flower has faded,
> And the moon is waning.

On the spur of the moment, the Vietnamese ambassador had moved the Imperial Court with his poetic eulogy, taking into account the four uniquenesses mentioned in the clue to the riddle. The entire diplomatic corps was startled by the brilliance of their Vietnamese colleague. The prestige of Vietnam was never so high in the literary firmament of China.

Literary Cold War

But the Vietnamese-Chinese literary cold war was not always conducted in a poetical or gentlemanly manner. From time to time, the Vietnamese court was tested on vulgar grounds, and the Vietnamese did not hesitate to answer in kind. At the beginning of the eighteenth century, the relations between China and Vietnam were strained. The Chinese tried to exploit the weaknesses of a divided and unstable Vietnam. Peking escalated its normal quota for tribute. Hitherto, tribute in gold or silver was not mandatory. But this time, China turned a leaf back in the history of past relations between the two countries and found out that at one time, in 1428, Emperor Le Loi (who had overthrown a ten-year-long Chinese domination after a protracted guerrilla war of national liberation) had sent to China as tribute two life-sized dummies in pure gold. One represented the Vietnamese emperor in person. He could not make the trip to Peking—or, more correctly, he did not want to go there. The other represented (with due apologies) a Chinese general named Liao Cheng, killed in an ambush by the Vietnamese guerrillas at the famous Chi Lang pass in North Vietnam. Based on this historical precedent, the Chinese demanded that a dummy in gold representing the person of the emperor be sent as part of the tribute. This condition had to be fulfilled unless the Vietnamese produced a buffalo that could defeat a huge Chinese fighting buffalo that the Chinese ambassador had brought along with him. The Chinese knew well that Vietnamese buffaloes were smaller, less aggressive. When the Vietnamese dignitaries had a look at the impressive Chinese beast, they had no doubt that the contest would be unfair. But the Chinese ultimatum would expire in three days. The first chancellor of the court suggested to the emperor that scholar Nguyen Quynh be called for advice in this time of national crisis. The Vietnamese emperor had heard of the controversial figure whom people called Cong Quynh, but he did not like him. Cong Quynh was known all over the land as the wittiest, the most arrogant, intellectually subversive, and obscene scholar. But the emperor had no choice. Cong Quynh was finally introduced to him. He listened attentively to the monarch's problem, then smiled and said: "Your Majesty, please do not worry. Your humble servant will have a successful answer to the Chinese ultimatum."

In the meantime, a strong wooden enclosure was built inside the imperial palace, leaving one single exit, through which the vanquished buffalo would flee. D-Day of the contest arrived. The Chinese ambassador, sitting next to the Vietnamese emperor, was amused to see that the Vietnamese challenger was just a baby buffalo, about the height of the legs of the Chinese giant. The Peking envoy laughed loudly, but not for too long. The Vietnamese buffalo, who had been separated from his mother for three days, drinking only water, was hungry for milk. At the sight of the male Chinese buffalo, the young Vietnamese buffalo rushed over, sniffing at the giant's penis, which he mistook to be a teat. The Chinese buffalo's surprise grew to annoyance and panic. He fled. The Chinese court quietly dropped its unreasonable demand.

The last Vietnamese diplomatic mission to China took place in 1813 under Emperor Gia Long (the founder, in 1802, of the Nguyen dynasty, of which ex-Emperor Bao Dai was the last descendant. The leader of this mission was a renowned poet, Nguyen Du. He came back from this trip with a Chinese story, from which he wrote the epic poem *Kim Van Kieu,* acclaimed ever since as the national poetic treasure of Vietnam.

With the French colonization of Vietnam in 1884, all formal relations between China and her southern neighbor ended. The literary cold war between the two countries was over. In many ways, this was most unfortunate, as it deprived the Vietnamese of invaluable anecdotes and poems that captivated the minds of the Vietnamese—the peasantry and the intellectuals—and strengthened their faith in the intellectual power of their nation.

"SAIGON: FROM CITADEL TO NATION'S CAPITAL," BY *Charles A. Joiner*, WITH *Nguyen Van Thuan* (Institute of Public Administration, Saigon)

The history of Saigon, the capital of South Vietnam, reflects the history of Vietnam. Initially a market town, it thrived in the nineteenth century, first under the rule of the Nguyen dynasty, then under the French. Prior to the nineteenth century, Vietnam had been ruled by two rival feudal houses, the Trinh in the North and the Nguyen in the South. Neither could conquer each other, so Vietnam remained administratively divided for more than a century. In the latter half of the eighteenth century, a rebellion led by the Tay Son brothers briefly united strife-torn Vietnam. It was not until 1802 that a Nguyen prince, Emperor Gia Long, reunited the country and established a strong, centralized administration. His heirs ruled throughout the French conquest; the last, Emperor Bao Dai, was deposed by referendum in 1956.

Prior to the Chinese and Vietnamese migrations, the current site of Saigon was named Prei-Nokor by the Khmers (the traditional name for Cambodia). Prei-Nokor served as the seat of a pretender, or second king, to the Cambodian throne. The next significant stage in the development of Saigon following the Chinese and Vietnamese migrations is closely tied to the political evolution in Vietnam during the eighteenth-century period of rapid switches in the fortunes of the house of Nguyen.

For over a century the houses of Trinh and Nguyen had skirmished for control of the nation, with the former predominant in the North (Tonkin) and the latter predominant in the South (Annam and later also Cochinchina). In 1771, a third house entered the competition, the Tay Son. Following the fall of Hue (in central Vietnam) to the Tay Son, the Nguyen fled southward, whereupon the Tay Son invaded Cochinchina. A series of successive periods of occupation of the Saigon area followed, with the Tay Son and the Nguyen each losing control on several occasions.

When the Tay Son invaded Bien Hoa in 1773, Chinese tradesmen residing and carrying on business in this area were forced to flee. The Chinese refugees from Bien Hoa finally settled, in 1778, in the area around the present site of Cholon, a suburb of present-day Saigon. They named their new residence Ta Ngon, or Tin Ngan. The Vietnamese pronunciation of the Chinese terms for the present Cholon sounded somewhat like "Saigon."

For the next several years after the conquest of Bien Hoa, the city changed hands frequently. Phan Yen Province (Gia Dinh) was attacked by the Tay Son in 1782, who marched into "Saigon" and massacred some 2,000 Chinese residents. This massacre resulted from the Tay Son fear of the increasing numbers of Chinese and of the dominance of the Chinese over trade throughout the entire region.

After Nguyen Anh [the Nguyen dynasty heir, who became Emperor Gia Long] fled to Phu Quoc Island, midway between Cape Ca Mau and the Gulf of Thailand, the Tay Son turned north to victory in Tonkin over the Trinh and later over a Trinh-Chinese coalition. Despite their significant victories, the Tay Son were weakened enough in the south due to quarrels among themselves to provide Nguyen Anh with an opportunity to first reconquer Gia Dinh (1788) and occupy Saigon (1789) and then to reunify the entire country. In 1802, he proclaimed himself to be the Emperor Gia Long. He once again established the capital in Hue and changed the name of the country from An Nam to Vietnam.

Vietnam was united. Many almost phenomenal successes followed during the reigns of the Emperor Gia Long (1802–19) and his successors Minh Mang (1820–40), Thien Tri (1841–49), and Tu Duc (1847–83). Both Cambodia and Laos became Vietnamese satellites despite certain interim setbacks for the Vietnamese forces.

A much stronger national government was established with a greatly improved military establishment, and a tightly knit centralization of authority based upon a hierarchical administrative network, wherein power originated in the person and office of the emperor and filtered through the mandarinal system and the village notables. Local governments lost most of the autonomy they historically enjoyed. Rapid advances were made in commerce, education, and administration. In short, the government of Vietnam following the fall of the Tay Son proved to be strong but despotic.

The French Move in

However, Gia Long had not returned from Phu Quoc Island to Hue without assistance. He had been aided by French troops recruited by the Bishop of Adran (Pigneau de Behaine of the Missions Etrangères de Paris), the Apostolic Delegate to South An Nam and later Royal Commissioner for South An Nam. After the French government withdrew from an agreement to aid Gia Long instigated at the bishop's insistence, he personally recruited French troops to aid Gia Long's return.

An important door had been opened, and later attempts to shut out the French proved increasingly futile. Gia Long permitted the Catholics to continue the proselytizing that had begun on a meager basis over two centuries before. He even stimulated a minimum amount of trade with the French, although successfully excluding other foreign traders.

Saigon thrived considerably between 1789, when Gia Long returned, and its conquest by the French in 1859. After vanquishing the Tay Son, Gia Long rebuilt the citadel, in 1790, with the assistance of the French troops recruited by Pigneau de Behaine, Bishop of Adran. The citadel was a fortress with eight gates surrounded by a highway encircled by a moat. It was an octagonal structure constructed on a hill. The center of the citadel was located on the site of the present Saigon Cathedral.

Built on Swamps

> The Saigon citadel was built with stone, by the side of an arsenal, sided by a civilian residential quarter including low, thatched houses. The commercial quarter faced the east. When Emperor Gia Long succeeded in defeating the Tay Son, the population returned in large numbers to the citadel and improved their dwellings and preferred to move to the west side of the citadel. By that time, the river and canal sides were paved with stones and brick for roughly one thousand meters. Some roads and streets were paved with stone but not well traced and maintained. The population of the citadel and its suburb was estimated to be about 180,000 Vietnamese and 10,000 Chinese. (*Extract from the notebook of an American traveler, John White, who visited Saigon in 1819.*)

Saigon became an important residential area for the Vietnamese in the South. The Chinese, during the long period of peace in Cochinchina after 1789, recovered their previous economic position and made Cholon the most important market for the six neighboring provinces. Even legal restrictions on many of their activities did not deter them from economic advancement. These restrictions were rarely enforced, chiefly because of bribery of the mandarins. The Chinese also expanded their activities and the facilities of Cholon without an abundance of financial support from the government, building roads and landing-piers and digging canals with their own investments.

When the French invaded Saigon in 1859, they completely demolished the new citadel. However, in 1860 they built an armored concrete fortification, the "*Caserne du Onzième Regiment de l'Infanterie Coloniale.*"

"LETTER OF PHAN THANH GIAN TO THE EMPEROR TU DUC" (in *La Geste Française en Indochine*, by *Georges Taboulet* [Paris, 1956]), translated by *Marjorie Weiner Normand* (Parentheses and ellipses are the author's)

Phan Thanh Gian, born in 1796 in the province of Ben Tre, was one of the few mandarins of Cochinchinese origin to attain the highest rank. He held many important posts during his lifetime and was a confidant of both emperors under whom he served: Minh Mang and Tu Duc. His brilliant career was terminated during the French conquest of Vietnam. He served as Tu Duc's envoy to France, always attempting to limit the extent of French intervention, but he was fighting a hopeless battle. After futile negotiations, he came to realize that resistance was useless and costly to the Vietnamese. At the French demand, he ceded the three provinces of Western Cochinchina, of which he was in charge, without a fight. He did this to spare his people useless suffering, but as a Confucian he felt that he had betrayed his sovereign, and he committed suicide.

Phan Thanh Gian was one of the few high mandarins who realized the senselessness of fighting the French with antiquated weapons and sensed the necessity of coming to terms with the modern world. His fellow mandarins led revolts against the French—always unsuccessfully—until the twentieth century. Phan Thanh Gian was both a realist and a philosopher; his letter to the emperor and his instructions to the mandarins, full of emotion yet restrained and dignified, urge adherence to the laws of nature and the will of Heaven.

8, July 1867

I, Phan Thanh Gian, make the (following) report, in expressing frankly, with my head bowed, my humble sentiments, and in soliciting, with my head raised, your discerning scrutiny.

During the period of difficulties and misfortunes that we are presently undergoing, rebellion is rising around the capital, the pernicious influence (the French intervention) is expanding on our frontiers. The territorial question is rapidly leading to a situation that it is impossible to end.

My duty compels me to die. I would not dare live thoughtlessly, leaving a heritage of shame to my Sovereign and my Father. Happily, I have confidence in my Emperor, who has extensive knowledge of ancient times and the present and who has studied profoundly the causes of peace and of dissention: . . . In respectfully observing the warnings of Heaven and in having pity on the misery of man . . . in changing the string (of the guitar), in modifying the track (of the governmental chariot), it is still possible for you to act in accordance with your authority and means.

At the last moment of life, the throat constricted, I do not know what to say, but, in wiping my tears and in raising my eyes toward you affectionately, I can only ardently hope (that this wish will be realized). With respect, I make this report, Tu Duc, twentieth year, sixth moon, seventh day, Phan Thanh Gian.

"THE LAST MESSAGE FROM PHAN THAN GIAN TO HIS ADMINISTRATORS" (in *La Geste Française en Indochine*, by *Georges Taboulet* [Paris, 1956]), translated by *Marjorie Weiner Normand* (parentheses and ellipses are the author's)

Mandarins and people,

It is written: He who lives in accordance with the will of Heaven lives in virtue; he who does not live according to the will of Heaven lives in evil. To work according to the will of Heaven is to listen to natural reason. . . . Man is an intelligent animal created by Heaven. Every animal lives according to his nature, as water flows to low ground, as fire goes out on dry ground. . . . Men, to whom Heaven has given reason, must apply themselves to live in obedience to this reason which Heaven has given them.

The empire of our king is ancient. Our gratitude toward our kings is complete and always ardent; we cannot forget them. Now, the French are come, with their powerful weapons of war to cause dissension among us. We are weak against them; our commanders and our soldiers have been vanquished. Each battle adds to our misery. . . . The French have immense warships, filled with soldiers and armed with huge cannons. No one can resist them. They go where they want, the strongest ramparts fall before them.

I have raised my spirit toward Heaven and I have listened to the voice of reason. And I have said: "It would be as senseless for you to wish to defeat your enemies by force of arms as for a young fawn to attack a tiger. You attract uselessly great misfortunes upon the people whom Heaven has confided to you. I have thus written to all the mandarins and to all the war commanders to break their lances and surrender the forts without fighting.

But, if I have followed the Will of Heaven by averting great evils from the head of the people, I am a traitor to our king in delivering without resistance the provinces which belong to him. . . . I deserve death. Mandarins and people, you can live under the command of the French, who are only terrible during the battle, but their flag must never fly above a fortress where Phan Thanh Gian still lives."

An aerial view of the old Citadel of Hue (*Photo: JUSPAO-Saigon*)

NATIONALISM AND COMMUNISM IN THE TWENTIETH CENTURY

"A HISTORICAL VIEW OF THE VIETNAMESE NATIONALIST CAUSE," BY *Senator Dan Van Sung*

This is an attempt to explain why non-Communist nationalists in Vietnam failed to lead the struggle against French colonial rule. Dan Van Sung examines Vietnamese nationalism in historic terms, when revolution was accomplished simply by gathering together an army and substituting a good ruler for an evil one.

A Harmonious Whole

Throughout our history, until a few decades ago, the Vietnamese nationalist cause was as clear as it was simple, because our society was organized in such a way as to make it natural for the Vietnamese to think of themselves as a harmonious whole. Under foreign domination, the nationalist cause meant ousting the invader. Under an evil king, it meant overthrowing the rotten men in power. In either case, if an uprising succeeded, the hero who had led the fight automatically began a new dynasty. In so doing, he would be satisfying the will of the people. Everybody accepted Confucianism as the philosophy of life, for the individual as well as for the society. The scholars, the leading social group, were born of the masses and remained in close contact with them. A scholar could become a mandarin or, if such was his inclination, stay at home and teach. The mandarin administered under the critical eye of the teacher who led public opinion. There was only one right way of governing. Any time there was a need of a change, it was merely a change of the men in power.

Sense of Duty

Under such conditions, a revolution had no need to be based on ideas but only on a strong sense of duty to and of sacrifice for the nation. And there were no two ways of carrying out a revolution: The revolutionist magnified and nourished his hatred against his enemy, secretly built up strength by gathering men and means, and when an opportunity came, loomed out of the darkness and killed. Once the enemy was put to death or chased away, the revolution was successful. One returned to the right way with the right man. From the Trung sisters in A.D. 40 to Phan Dinh Phung toward the end of the nineteenth century, the legitimate cause was the same, the policy the same, and the behavior, methods, and technique all the same. This long tradition deeply impressed the Vietnamese revolutionist mind. Even today, it is still reflected in the thought and action of many, chiefly among men of a certain age. That is unfortunate, because Vietnam has probably changed more in the last three decades than in the previous twenty centuries.

With the twentieth century, various social doctrines came to the attention of the revolutionary scholars. But the French were so strong, the colonialist regime so firmly entrenched that any social or political reform could only take place in the remote realm of a dream. With the feeble means available to us, the antinationalist stronghold seemed invulnerable. The famous slogan of Nguyen Thai Hoc, the leader of the Viet-nam Quoc Dan Dang [Nationalist Party], expressed the general spirit as well as the general feeling among the Vietnamese nationalists of the moment. "Even if we shall not succeed, we shall have done our duty." Moved by this same sense of duty and sacrifice, he led a desperate uprising and went to the scaffold (1930), only to show the unconquerable spirit of the Vietnamese.

Independence Comes First

After Nguyen Thai Hoc, the various nationalist groups felt the necessity to move with the times, both ideologically and technically. Each group adopted a political and social viewpoint and had a program. But it is only honest to recognize that the program existed only in form but not yet in substance, more as an expediency or an imitation of other countries than through a mature and thoughtful conviction based on an actual study of realities. Anyhow, a nationalist at that time joined his party in order to fight the French and cared little for the party's doctrine. "Independence first. As for which political and social system to adopt after independence, there would be enough time later to think about that in detail." In comparison with the times of Nguyen Thai Hoc, the nationalists by 1945 were numerically much stronger—in the form of many clandestine groups—but they were hardly more advanced in revolutionary thought, knowledge, and technique. The conditions of the fight, on the contrary, had greatly changed.

The Crisis of the Nationalist Cause in 1945

Given their limitations at the time, the Vietnamese nationalists were not ready to cope with the situation confronting them in 1945. The opportunity to fight for independence came after the war, but not under the same conditions as had existed previously. Before the nationalists were ready to chase out the invader, another enemy appeared in the form of the Communists. This enemy came from within. For the first time, all Vietnamese revolutionists no longer thought of the Vietnamese people as an absolute whole. The problem of emancipation of the individual now became a real factor in the fight for the emancipation of the people. In order to remain a nationalist, the nationalist now had to have a clear-cut political viewpoint, which he did not have.

An Élan Captured by the Left

To my mind, the Communist assumption of the leadership of the resistance movement is the real cause of the division of Vietnam after a long and murderous war, and explains why half of our country is still under a Communist regime. Vietnam was within the sphere of the anti-Communist world. If the nationalists had led the fight against the French—as they logically should have done—Vietnam would have gained its independence, and the country would have remained whole, just like the other countries in the Far East.

The damage caused by the initial mistake went still further. It led to the division of the Vietnamese patriots into two antagonistic groups actively engaged in killing each other. After this mistake, the nationalist parties first lost their influence upon the population, then their anti-French, anti-colonialist unanimity. The great majority of patriots who could have been expected to join the nationalist parties, had these parties been leading the fight, now had no alternative but to go to those who fought: the Viet Minh. By enrolling them, the Communists won their victory over the French with the blood of their potential enemies in the establishment of a Communist regime after independence. Save a few, those who managed to escape are now an unhappy lot in a false position among the nationalists.

As for the nationalist parties, their basic mistake was their death blow. The moment the Communists fired the first shot of the resistance, all the nationalists were paralyzed. When the war began between the colonialists and the Communists, there was no room left anywhere for the nationalists. Even nationalist thought reached an impasse: To fight against the French would serve the Communists, to fight the Communists would serve the colonialists. The dilemma of nationalist thought was illustrated by the alternatives that the nationalists saw open to them. The first was an attitude called *attentisme*, adopted throughout the resistance period by a number of nationalist parties and by most of the "intellectuals." It was the negative attitude of doing nothing and waiting for something to happen in the future. Second, some nationalist parties remained active in allying themselves with the French against the Communists while fighting for independence through political means. There might be some logic in such an attitude: The dying French imperialism was less to be feared than the rising Communist one. But such was not the view of the masses: independence first, the Communist problem to be solved afterwards.

Mistake

Nationalist thought and behavior was also affected in another way. The Communist superiority in organizational technique was too obvious for the nationalists not to be aware of it. In order to match it, it became necessary for the nationalists to develop their own technique. But instead of trying to learn and develop, a number of nationalists succumbed to the tendency of copying the Communists' behavior, method, and technique in dealing not with the Communists but with one another. This did little harm to the Communists but caused much damage to the nationalists themselves. It seriously weakened their traditional scruples and moral strength.

Such was the price the Vietnamese nationalists had to pay for failing to hold fast to the legitimate goal of their fight: revolution and independence.

"HOW THE COMMUNISTS CAPTURED THE NATIONALIST REVOLUTION," BY *Marjorie Weiner Normand*

In the early years of the twentieth century, Vietnamese nationalists began to move away from traditional leaders—the mandarins—to focus on modern methods of achieving their goal of self-rule. They were influenced by exciting things happening in Asia: In 1905, the colossus of Russia was defeated by "little" Japan, the first time that a European nation was beaten by a well-trained and equipped Asian country. In 1911, Sun Yat-sen overthrew the tottering Manchu dynasty in China, amid high hopes that his government would democratize and modernize Vietnam's great northern neighbor.

In Vietnam, French intransigence and unwillingness to grant even a modicum of political representation to their subject people spelled the doom of efforts to work within the colonial framework to achieve reform. Instead, clandestine organizations, forced underground by the severity of the secret police, took up the banner of nationalism. They espoused violence as a means of achieving the ultimate goal—independence from France. These organizations multiplied in the 1920's and 1930's but were each decimated in turn by the repressive colonial administration.

Only one organization was able to make headway on a national basis, despite the ban on political activity: the Indochinese Communist Party (ICP) organized by Ho Chi Minh (then operating under the pseudonym Nguyen Ai Quoc) in 1930. It, too, had enormous difficulties because of constant surveillance, and most of the veteran leaders in Hanoi today did a turn in French colonial jails. However, the Party did manage to survive, and some of its mystique today derives from its claim of "leading the revolution since 1930." It is certainly a tribute to its organizational discipline and flexibility that the ICP was able to survive French repressive policies with its underground apparatus intact.

At the outbreak of World War II, most surviving nationalist leaders fled to southern China, while a Vichy-appointed governor-general in Indochina made a deal with the Japanese, enabling the French to maintain at least the appearance of authority over Vietnam. In line with Comintern policy advocating the formation of united fronts encompassing the widest possible spectrum of nationalist organizations, the ICP convoked a meeting of nationalist leaders and groups in southern China in May, 1941. Under the guidance of Ho Chi Minh, a front group was formed for the stated purpose of freeing Vietnam from foreign domination and achieving independence. Ho Chi Minh was made secretary general of this coalition, named the Vietnam Doc Lap Dong Minh Hoi (League for the Independence of Vietnam), popularly known as the Viet Minh.

The Japanese ruled Vietnam indirectly until March 9, 1945, when they executed a coup to destroy the façade of French government. Up until then, the Viet Minh had concentrated on securing a political base in the northernmost provinces of Vietnam, bordering on China. Communist cadres had begun to propagandize in the villages of the mountain areas, and Vo Nguyen Giap, a former history teacher and member of the ICP, had been training guerrilla forces and starting a Liberation Army. The sudden disappearance of French authority in the countryside in 1945 provided enormous impetus to the revolutionary movement, and the Viet Minh, with unusual energy and efficiency, capitalized on the situation. Teams of cadres were sent into the Red River Delta itself to transform villages into "liberation bases" and recruit for the Liberation Army. Feverish preparations were made for a final takeover.

When the Japanese suddenly capitulated on August 13, 1945, only the Viet Minh was ready with a plan of action. Other nationalist groups had remained in southern China under the protection of the Kuomintang or were operating in Vietnam in only a very limited way. Viet Minh leaders were determined to move into the power vacuum and present the Allies—and the Vietnamese people—with a *fait accompli* before opposition could arise either internally or internationally. Viet Minh soldiers raced into Hanoi and took over the administrative buildings there and in other cities in the North. A provisional government was named at a hastily summoned national congress, and the call went out for a national insurrection. In the South, Viet Minh control was much weaker: Cochinchina was far from the Viet Minh base of operations, and there was strong competition from other national organizations, which balked at accepting Viet Minh leadership of an anti-French revolution.

Faced with this determined and militant organization claiming to lead a national movement for independence, the Emperor Bao Dai abdicated in favor of the Viet Minh–sponsored provisional government. On September 2, Ho Chi Minh, as president of the provisional government, read a declaration of independence to a vast crowd in Ba Dinh Square, Hanoi, and proclaimed the birth of the Democratic Republic of Vietnam.

Shortly thereafter, the situation became much more difficult for the provisional government. Allied forces were dispatched to Vietnam to disarm the Japanese: the Chinese north of the Sixteenth Parallel, and the British to the south. With British aid, French forces evicted the revolutionary movement from Saigon and began an attempt to "pacify" the South. In the North, the French faced a stronger nationalist organization running its own government and a Chinese army hostile to French colonial aspirations. They therefore came to terms with the Viet Minh–run Democratic Republic of Vietnam (DRV) on March 6, 1946, recognizing it as a "free state" within the French Union. This agreement was doomed, however, as French colonialists pushed for a reconquest and Vietnamese militants agitated for complete independence.

The war began in December, 1946, and Vietnamese nationalists of all political persuasions rallied to the Viet Minh banner and the cause of independence. The outbreak of war sealed Viet Minh leadership of the nationalist revolution, but it was won primarily by the "August Revolution," as that month of extraordinary initiative and action came to be known in Communist mythology.

ABDICATION STATEMENT, BY HIS MAJESTY BAO DAI (in *The Democratic Republic of Vietnam* [Information Service, Vietnam Delegation in France, 1948])

At the end of World War II, the Japanese granted "independence" to a government headed by the Emperor Bao Dai. However, effective control over the countryside had passed to a nationalist movement headed by the Viet Minh. Therefore, Bao Dai agreed to abdicate on August 26, 1945. In so doing, he handed over the reins of government to the Viet Minh–sponsored provisional government of the Democratic Republic of Vietnam, and urged his countrymen to rally to the cause of independence. He also accepted the post of Supreme Political Advisor in the new government, thus providing it with an important symbol of legitimacy.

For the happiness of the Vietnamese peoples, and for the independence of Vietnam,

We declare ourself ready to make all sacrifices, in the hope that such sacrifices will be of benefit to the Nation.

Conscious that the union of our compatriots at this moment is an absolute necessity for our Fatherland, We solemnly warned our people on August 22nd: "At this decisive moment in the nation's history, unity is life, and division death."

In view of the mighty democratic forces released in the north of our Realm, We were at first apprehensive lest conflict between the North and South should be inevitable, if We were to await the opening of a National Congress before taking a decision; and We were aware that this conflict, should it occur, would entail much suffering for our peoples besides giving a golden opportunity to the invader to despoil our territory.

We cannot escape some feeling of melancholic frustration at the thought of the achievements of our glorious ancestors who fought without respite for 400 years to extend the frontiers of our country from Thuan-hoa to Ha-tien;

Neither can We help feeling a certain regret in looking back on our twenty-year-old reign, during which our position has been such that it was well-nigh impossible for Us to render any appreciable service to our Country.

Notwithstanding this, We firmly decide to abdicate our throne, and We hand over Sovereign power to the Democratic Republic of Vietnam.

In so doing, We have but three wishes to express:

(1) We request the New Government to take care of the dynastic temples and royal tombs;

(2) We request the New Government to treat in a spirit of fraternity all parties and groups who have fought for the independence of the country, even though they may not have closely followed the popular movement; so that they may have the opportunity to participate in the reconstruction of the country, and proof be given that the new regime is founded upon the absolute union of the entire people;

(3) We call upon all parties and groups, all classes of society as well as the Royal Family to strengthen and support unreservedly the Democratic Republic of Vietnam, in order to consolidate our national independence.

As for Us, We have known great bitterness during the twenty years of our rule. Henceforth, we are happy to assume the status of a free citizen in an independent country. We shall allow no one to abuse our name or that of the Royal Family to sow discord among our compatriots.

Long live the independence of Vietnam!

Long live our Democratic Republic!

Hue, August 26th, 1945
Signed: BAO DAI

"PROCLAMATION OF BAO DAI," September 18, 1947 (in *Notes Documentaires et Études*, October 30, 1947, Services Français d'Information), translated by *Marjorie Weiner Normand*

It is interesting to compare Bao Dai's abdication message with the following proclamation, issued after Bao Dai had gone into exile. With the outbreak of war between French troops and the Viet

Minh in December, 1946, French authorities began to seek a Vietnamese political alternative to the Democratic Republic of Vietnam. They approached Bao Dai, and he agreed to return to Saigon as Chief of State of the State of Vietnam. This was the beginning of the two Vietnams. Bao Dai's government, however, never succeeded in attracting many nationalists away from the Viet Minh cause; and among those who refused to work with the Communists, many also remained alienated from Bao Dai's pro-French government, prefering to "wait and see," an attitude the French called attentisme. *Bao Dai's failure stemmed in large part from France's unwillingness to grant him what had been refused Ho Chi Minh: unity and independence for Vietnam.*

"Vietnamese People! In order to avoid shedding the blood of my compatriots, I would renounce the throne of my fathers. You wished to confide the responsibility of your destiny to new rulers so I voluntarily removed myself. I abdicated and took the path of exile in order not to be an obstacle to that experience which you thought would bring you happiness. I went to exile in a foreign country, where I still am. I can follow sometimes with hope and often with sadness the development of these recent and terrible pages of our history. I am not unaware of any of your hopes. I follow your torments, your suffering. Despite the dictatorship that is trying to stifle your voice, I hear today your appeals and cries of distress. You delineate for me the state of your misery and make out the account of disasters suffered by our dear Vietnam after two years of experience during which your rulers exercised absolute power. Thus, little by little, the hopes of happiness that clever propaganda had created in your hearts for a moment, vanished. In your distress, you came to me. You appealed to my authority to re-establish peace in our country, ravaged by war and torn by internal dissention, a peace appropriate to free and equal States, a peace with interior security. You solicited me to be your negotiator with France, which asked you, through the voice of its very important representative in Vietnam, the High Commissioner Bollaert, in his speech at Ha Dong, to designate individuals having your confidence.

Responding to your call, I accept the mission that you entrust to me and am ready to enter into contact with French authorities.

With them, I will examine with all objectivity the proposals which will be made to us. I wish, first of all, to obtain independence and unity in accordance with your aspirations, to arrive at agreements on reciprocal guarantees, and to be able to declare to you that the ideal for which you have battled with such fierce resistance is indeed reached. Thus, I will use my authority to arbitrate this conflict that has set you all against each other, since once our goal is reached, nothing must stand in the way of the return of peace.

This generative peace, the prosperity and security that it will give us, I wish you to preserve. Time will heal the suffering. In union, we Vietnamese will rebuild our beautiful country on new foundations, drawing our main strength from our mighty traditions.

PROCLAMATION OF THE REPUBLIC (October 26, 1955), BY *Ngo Dinh Diem* (in *Vietnam in World Affairs* [Secretariat of State for Foreign Affairs, Saigon, December, 1955])

At the time of the Geneva Conference, the Emperor Bao Dai, then Chief of State of the State of Vietnam, named Ngo Dinh Diem as Premier. Those were dark days for South Vietnam, and Diem was beset by problems from all sides. He managed to gain control of the army, subdue the rival politico-military sects, and impose his authority on the administration. On October 23, 1955, the people of Vietnam in a referendum deposed Bao Dai as Chief of State and elected Ngo Dinh Diem to succeed him. Here is Ngo Dinh Diem's proclamation of the Republic, on October 26, 1955.

Fellow Countrymen,

A year ago, with the anguish that was in our hearts, who among us could have foreseen that we would, in the not too distant future, finally extricate ourselves from an impossible and almost desperate situation?

But in the darkest hours of our history, our people have always joined together and now, in a moment of supreme unity, we have broken the bands of iron and fire that encircled us, taking the path toward independence and liberty.

In the terrible battle that men and women, both military and civilian, have waged for more than a year against interior as well as exterior forces, this same unity of feeling has allowed us to liquidate an outdated regime. The focus of our national interest has been placed in the South, where hope for a better future for every human being was born. It is this new hope which drew a million refugees to us from the North, and their presence among us further reinforces our confidence in the righteousness of our cause.

Compatriots, the October 23rd plebiscite in which you took such an enthusiastic part constitutes an approval of the policies pursued thus far and, at the same time, augurs a whole new era for the future of our country.

The new responsibilities which you entrust me today—to

form a democracy in our beloved country—are heavy for my shoulders, alone, however.

Democracy is not a group of texts and laws, to be read and applied. It is essentially a state of mind, a way of living with the utmost respect toward every human being, ourselves as well as our neighbors. It requires constant self-education, careful practice, flexible and patient attention, in order to achieve a harmonious balance between the desirably diverse conceptions of men and the inevitable complexity of reality. Democracy demands from each of us, then, infinitely more efforts, understanding, and good will than any other form of government.

Confident in the unity that you proved during the difficult times we endured, confident in the moral strength of our people whose spirit has been enriched by elements from the oldest and most highly developed civilizations, I know that together we will be able to throw off all forms of oppression and to build the ideal political and economic state to which our people aspire with such fervor.

Compatriots, it is in this spirit that the constitution of our country will be written and the members of our National Assembly elected.

On the threshold of this new era which presages true democracy for Vietnam, let us ask for divine guidance for our country, and let us reverently remember all those who, long ago or only recently, made the supreme sacrifice in order that we might lead free and independent lives.

Let us express our gratitude toward the friendly countries who, even in the darkest hours of our struggle, had faith in us and in our eventual success.

United and determined, we shall see a unified, free, and prosperous Vietnam emerge triumphantly.

With this conviction, and following the desires you expressed by your vote of October 23, 1955, I solemnly proclaim that the State of Vietnam is a Republic.

PREAMBLE, CONSTITUTION OF THE DEMOCRATIC REPUBLIC OF VIETNAM (in *Constitution of the Democratic Republic of Vietnam* [Hanoi, 1960])

When peace came to North Vietnam in 1954, the government of the Democratic Republic of Vietnam (DRV) embarked on an ambitious program of reconstruction of the war-devastated country. By 1960, it felt strong enough to initiate an ambitious five-year economic plan geared to lay the material and technical foundations of socialism.

At the same time, the DRV adopted a new constitution providing the foundations for a centralized regime with strong national powers. Unlike its predecessor, adopted in 1946, the new constitution was written to govern only the North and to bring it to socialism. However, Article I affirms: "The territory of Vietnam is a single, indivisible whole from North to South." The constitution of the Republic of Vietnam says much the same thing; no Vietnamese government would long survive if it did not espouse reunification.

This preamble provides a capsule version of the DRV's political and social goals, as well as a Communist view of Vietnam's modern history.

Vietnam is a single entity from Lang Son to Camau.

The Vietnamese people, throughout their thousands of years of history, have been an industrious working people who have struggled unremittingly and heroically to build their country and to defend the independence of their fatherland.

Throughout more than eighty years of French colonial rule and five years of occupation by the Japanese fascists, the Vietnamese people consistently united and struggled against domination by the foreign aggressors in order to liberate their country.

From 1930 onward, under the leadership of the Indochinese Communist Party—now the Vietnam Lao Dong Party—the Vietnamese revolution advanced into a new stage. The persistent struggle, full of hardship and heroic sacrifice, of our people against imperialist and feudal domination won great success: the August Revolution was victorious, the Democratic Republic of Vietnam was founded, and, on September 2, 1945, President Ho Chi Minh proclaimed Vietnam's independence to the people and the world. For the first time in their history, the Vietnamese people had founded an independent and democratic Vietnam.

On January 6, 1946, the entire Vietnamese people, from North to South, enthusiastically took part in the first general elections to the National Assembly. The National Assembly adopted the first constitution, which clearly recorded the great success of our people and highlighted the determination of the entire nation to safeguard the independence and unity of the Fatherland and to defend the freedom and democratic rights of the people.

However, the French imperialists, assisted by the U.S. imperialists, again provoked an aggressive war in an attempt to seize our country and once more enslave our people. Under the leadership of the Vietnamese working-class party and the Government of the Democratic Republic of Vietnam, our entire people, united as one, rose to fight the aggressors and save their country. At the same time, our people carried out land rent-reduction and land reform with the aim of overthrowing the landlord class, and restoring the land to those who till it. The long, hard, and extremely heroic war of resistance of the Vietnamese people, which enjoyed the sympathy and support of the socialist countries, of the oppressed peoples and of friends of peace throughout the world, won glorious victory. With the Dien Bien Phu victory, the Vietnamese people defeated the French imperialists and the U.S. interventionists. The 1954 Geneva agreements were concluded: Peace was restored in Indochina on the basis of recognition of the independence, sovereignty, unity, and territorial integrity of our country.

This major success of the Vietnamese people was also a common success of the liberation movement of the oppressed peoples, of the world front of peace and of the socialist camp.

Since the restoration of peace, in completely liberated North Vietnam, our people have carried through the national people's democratic revolution. But the South is still under the rule of the imperialists and feudalists; our country is still temporarily divided into two zones.

The Vietnamese revolution has moved into a new position. Our people must endeavor to consolidate the North, taking it toward socialism; and to carry on the struggle for peaceful reunification of the country and completion of the tasks of the national people's democratic revolution throughout the country.

In the last few years, our people in the North have achieved many big successes in economic rehabilitation and cultural development. At present, socialist transformation and construction are being successfully carried out.

Meanwhile, in the South, the U.S. imperialists and their henchmen have been savagely repressing the patriotic movement of our people. They have been strengthening military forces and carrying out their scheme of turning the southern part of our country into a colony and military base for their war preparations. They have resorted to all possible means to sabotage the Geneva agreements and undermine the cause of Vietnam's reunification. But our southern compatriots have constantly struggled heroically and refused to submit to them. The people throughout the country, united as one, are holding aloft the banner of peace, national unity, independence, and democracy, resolved to march forward and win final victory. The cause of the peaceful reunification of the Fatherland will certainly be victorious.

In the new stage of the revolution, our National Assembly must amend the 1946 constitution in order to adapt it to the new situation and tasks.

The new constitution clearly records the great revolutionary gains in the recent past and clearly indicates the goal of struggle of our people in the new stage.

Our State is a people's democratic State based on the alliance between the workers and peasants and led by the working class. The new constitution defines the political, economic, and social system of our country, the relations of equality and mutual assistance among the various nationalities in our country, and provides for the taking of the North toward socialism, the constant improvement of the material and cultural life of the people and the building of a stable and strong North Vietnam as a basis for the struggle for the peaceful reunification of the country.

The new constitution defines the responsibilities and powers of the State organs and the rights and duties of citizens, with a view to developing the great creative potentialities of our people in national construction and in the reunification and defense of the fatherland.

The new constitution is a genuinely democratic constitution. It is a force inspiring the people throughout our country to march forward enthusiastically and win new successes. Our people are resolved to develop further their patriotism, their tradition of solidarity, their determination to struggle, and their ardor in work. Our people are resolved to strengthen further solidarity and unity of mind with the brother countries in the socialist camp headed by the great Soviet Union, and to strengthen solidarity with the peoples of Asia and Africa and peace-loving people all over the world.

Under the clearsighted leadership of the Vietnam Lao Dong Party, the Government of the Democratic Republic of Vietnam and President Ho Chi Minh, our entire people, broadly united within the National United Front, will surely win glorious success in the building of socialism in North Vietnam and the struggle for national reunification. Our people will surely be successful in building a peaceful, unified, independent, democratic, prosperous, and strong Vietnam, making a worthy contribution to the safeguarding of peace in Southeast Asia and the world.

VIETNAMESE LEADERS IN MODERN HISTORY

"PRESIDENT NGO DINH DIEM'S POLITICAL PHILOSOPHY," BY *Phuc Thien* (in *Ngo Dinh Diem of Vietnam* [Saigon: Press Office, Presidency of the Republic of Vietnam, 1957])

Ngo Dinh Diem, a former mandarin to the court of the Emperor Bao Dai, was invested with the office of Premier of the State of Vietnam by Bao Dai on June 17, 1954. He took over the reins of government in the South at a critical time. The Geneva conference was to result in the partition of the country; Catholic refugees were to pour South by the hundreds of thousands; the administration, the financial, social, and political systems were all in disarray. And forces within the South—private armies, even the national army—were threatening to destroy the government. But Diem took hold, and, with massive infusions of American aid and his own iron determination, was able to impose his authority on the government. He ruled for nine years, deposing Bao Dai, transforming South Vietnam into a republic, and waging war on the revolutionary movement in the South. His own traditional background and personal rigidity, however, made him unwilling or unable to institute the drastic reforms needed by his administration, and he successively alienated a good part of the population of his country. Opposition to his repressive policies brought about his final downfall in 1963, but his policies and programs have shaped the course of Vietnamese history to this day. His marks the last strong, purely civilian government that South Vietnam has had.

The main lines of President Ngo Dinh Diem's life are generally well known. Born in 1901 of an old Catholic family of mandarins, he grew up in both the traditional and the Catholic atmosphere. His father, the late Ngo Dinh Kha, was educated both at home and in Malaya. This fact is noteworthy. Few, if any men of Ngo Dinh Kha's generation had enough foresight to understand the necessity of acquiring knowledge beyond the borders of Vietnam.

For schooling, Ngo Dinh Kha sent his son to Pellerin School in Hue, where President Ngo Dinh Diem went through a system of both French and Vietnamese education.

Later, President Ngo Dinh Diem attended the National College, where both French and Vietnamese higher learning was dispensed. This college was founded through the initiative of his father, who saw the need for Vietnamese mandarins to be acquainted with Western ideas.

It goes without saying that, in his home, as in all families of his time, the father was a direct teacher to his children of Chinese classics. President Ngo Dinh Diem therefore was well grounded in both Western and traditional cultures.

What was perhaps unique about the education of President Ngo Dinh Diem is his acquaintance, at an early age, with men and ideas in an age of revolution. His father's home was the meeting place of all the political figures of the time: Emperor Thanh Thai, Emperor Duy Tan, Phan Boi Chau,

Phan Chu Trinh, Cuong De, and many others who came to enlist Ngo Dinh Kha's support or seek his advice.

Ngo Dinh Kha's stand, however, was unshakable: He would not hear of bloodshed or violent revolution. Revolution must come through the education of the people. When Vietnam had enough technicians of all kinds in all fields, then revolution would come of itself. Ngo Dinh Kha would not let himself be talked into joining revolutionary movements. But he would not hold the impatient back if he could not convince them of the vanity of their agitation. He would only shake his head sadly.

President Ngo Dinh Diem, then a young boy, was present at many of these discussions. He would sit and listen, and there is no doubt that these discussions had a tremendous impact on his mind. His father, too, never missed an opportunity to impress upon his children the necessity of education as a means to national revolution.

Another unique feature in President Ngo Dinh Diem's education is the insistence of his father that his brothers and he should learn to know the people whom they later were to lead. And the best method for doing this is to go out to watch the people work and live and work among them.

No Vietnamese statesman or politician has had this experience. President Ngo Dinh Diem's successes are due to a very large extent to this thorough knowledge of the people.

Unlike many of the present Vietnamese politicians, President Ngo Dinh Diem was not educated abroad or in a completely Western school. He always maintained contact with Vietnamese reality. Yet, as a boy, his father's stories stirred his imagination. He was a tireless reader, especially of history and geography. Later, he had to give up a scholarship in France, because as the eldest of the remaining children—his brother Ngo Dinh Thus was in a seminary at Quang Tri, and his brother Ngo Dinh Khoi was to leave for France—he had to look after his younger brothers and sisters and aging father. But he was seething with the desire to visit foreign lands.

The opportunity was given to him a great deal later, in 1948, when he went to Hong Kong to give advice to Bao Dai, and again, in 1950, when he accompanied his brother Ngo Dinh Thuc on a world tour that took him to Japan, the Philippines, the United States, and Europe. Everywhere, he worked as much as he studied.

The psychologists would tell us that the ideas of a man cannot be grafted on his mind overnight but are the results of a long process of study and influences. It is in this light that we have to understand President Ngo Dinh Diem's ideas. He certainly had a solid education and was better prepared than any other statesman to carry out the task of leading his country through a period of political as well as intellectual and moral crisis. More than any other Vietnamese statesman, President Ngo Dinh Diem understood the real causes of sickness of his country, and more than any other statesman he knew where to look for the new strength that would carry Vietnam through this period of crisis.

The remedy, for him, does not lie in any imported solution, ideas, or force. It is in the people themselves that we should look for it, for he firmly believes that although the country had been living on its reserves of moral strength for many decades, there are enough of them left to carry it over this period of difficulties.

On accepting office, he issued a statement on June 16, 1954, in which he declared: "I have faith in my people. I am convinced of its unsurmountable dislike for the lies and oppressions of dictatorial regimes. I have faith in its deepest love for freedom."

It is often said that men make history. But history also makes men. President Ngo Dinh Diem is certainly as much a genius in his own right as the fruit of his time. And that is why he has been successful where others failed.

EXCHANGE OF MESSAGES BETWEEN PRESIDENT JOHN F. KENNEDY AND PRESIDENT NGO DINH DIEM OF THE REPUBLIC OF VIETNAM, December 7 and December 14, 1961 (in U.S. Department of State *Bulletin*, January 1, 1962)

In 1960, the National Liberation Front (NLF) was formed to give shape and direction to a guerrilla war already being waged in the South against the government of Ngo Dinh Diem. The tactics of the NLF included the selective use of terror against local government officials, teachers, and so on, to weaken the hold of the central authority at the grass-roots level. By 1961, the level of violence had risen sharply and the Diem regime's power in the countryside had waned commensurately. Alarmed that the Communist movement in the South would succeed in destroying the Saigon regime by force, President Kennedy, in this exchange of letters with President Diem, pledged increased military assistance to Vietnam's defense effort. As the war escalated continually, the American effort also mounted until it reached massive levels.

The letter from President Diem illustrates his firm stand against what he considered the forces of "international Communism" seeking to destroy his country.

President Diem to President Kennedy

December 7, 1961

Dear Mr. President: Since its birth, more than six years ago, the Republic of Vietnam has enjoyed the close friendship and cooperation of the United States of America.

Like the United States, the Republic of Vietnam has always been devoted to the preservation of peace. My people know only too well the sorrows of war. We have honored the 1954 Geneva agreements, even though they resulted in the partition of our country and the enslavement of more than half of our people by Communist tyranny. We have never considered the reunification of our nation by force. On the contrary, we have publicly pledged that we will not violate the demarcation line and the demilitarized zone set up by the agreements. We have always been prepared and have on many occasions stated our willingness to reunify Vietnam on the basis of democratic and truly free elections.

The record of the Communist authorities in the northern part of our country is quite otherwise. They not only consented to the division of Vietnam, but were eager for it. They pledged themselves to observe the Geneva agreements and during the seven years since have never ceased to violate them. They call for free elections but are ignorant of the very meaning of the words. They talk of "peaceful reunification" and wage war against us.

From the beginning, the Communists resorted to terror in their efforts to subvert our people, destroy our government, and impose a Communist regime upon us. They have attacked defenseless teachers, closed schools, killed members of our antimalarial program, and looted hospitals. This is coldly calculated to destroy our government's humanitarian efforts to serve our people.

We have long sought to check the Communist attack from the North on our people by appeals to the International Control Commission (ICC). Over the years, we have repeatedly published to the world the evidence of the Communist plot to overthrow our government and seize control of all of Vietnam by illegal intrusions from outside our country. The evidence has mounted until now it is hardly necessary to rehearse it. Most recently, the kidnapping and brutal murder of our chief liaison officer to the International Control Commission, Colonel Hoang Thuy Nam, compelled us to speak out once more. In our October 24, 1961, letter to the ICC, we called attention again to the publicly stated determination of the Communist authorities in Hanoi to "liberate the South" by the overthrow of my government and the imposition of a Communist regime on our people. We cited the proof of massive infiltration of Communist agents and military elements into our country. We outlined the Communist strategy, which is simply the ruthless use of terror against the whole population, women and children included.

In the course of the last few months, the Communist assault on my people has achieved high ferocity. In October, they caused more than 1,800 incidents of violence and more than 2,000 casualties. They have struck occasionally in battalion strength, and they are continually augmenting their forces by infiltration from the North. The level of their attacks is already such that our forces are stretched to the utmost. We are forced to defend every village, every hamlet, indeed, every home against a foe whose tactic is always to strike at the defenseless.

A disastrous flood was recently added to the misfortunes of the Vietnamese people. The greater part of three provinces was inundated, with a great loss of property. We are now engaged in a nationwide effort to reconstruct and rehabilitate this area. The Communists are, of course, making this task doubly difficult, for they have seized upon the disruption of normal administration and communications as an opportunity to sow more destruction in the stricken area.

In short, the Vietnamese nation now faces what is perhaps the gravest crisis in its long history. For more than 2,000 years, my people have lived and built, fought and died in this land. We have not always been free. Indeed, much of our history and many of its proudest moments have arisen from conquest by foreign powers and our struggle against great odds to regain or defend our precious independence. But it is not only our freedom which is at stake today, it is our national identity. For if we lose this war, our people will be swallowed by the Communist bloc, all our proud heritage will be blotted out by the "socialist society," and Vietnam will leave the pages of history. We will lose our national soul.

Mr. President, my people and I are mindful of the great assistance that the United States has given us. Your help has not been lightly received, for the Vietnamese are proud people, and we are determined to do our part in the defense of the free world. It is clear to all of us that the defeat of the Viet Cong demands the total mobilization of our government and our people, and you may be sure that we will devote all of our resources of money, minds, and men to this great task.

But Vietnam is not a great power, and the forces of international Communism now arrayed against us are more than we can meet with the resources at hand. We must have further assistance from the United States if we are to win the war now being waged against us.

We can certainly assure mankind that our action is purely defensive. Much as we regret the subjugation of more than half of our people in North Vietnam, we have no intention, and indeed no means, to free them by use of force.

I have said that Vietnam is at war. War means many things, but most of all it means the death of brave people for a cause they believe in. Vietnam has suffered many wars, and through the centuries we have always had patriots and heroes who were willing to shed their blood for Vietnam. We will keep faith with them.

When Communism has long ebbed away into the past, my people will still be here, a free, united nation growing from the deep roots of our Vietnamese heritage. They will remember your help in our time of need. This struggle will then be a part of our common history. And your help, your friendship, and the strong bonds between our two peoples will be a part of Vietnam, then as now.

Signed: Ngo Dinh Diem

President Kennedy to President Diem

December 14, 1961

Dear Mr. President: I have received your recent letter in which you described so cogently the dangerous condition caused by North Vietnam's efforts to take over your country. The situation in your embattled country is well known to me and to the American people. We have been deeply disturbed by the assault on your country. Our indignation has mounted as the deliberate savagery of the Communist program of assassination, kidnapping, and wanton violence became clear.

Your letter underlines what our own information has convincingly shown—that the campaign of force and terror now being waged against your people and your Government is supported and directed from the outside by the authorities at Hanoi. They have thus violated the provisions of the Geneva Accords designed to ensure peace in Vietnam and to which they bound themselves in 1954.

At that time, the United States, although not a party to the Accords, declared that it "would view any renewal of the aggression in violation of the agreements with grave concern and as seriously threatening international peace and security." We continue to maintain that view.

In accordance with that declaration, and in response to your request, we are prepared to help the Republic of Vietnam to protect its people and to preserve its independence. We shall promptly increase our assistance to your defense effort as well as help relieve the destruction of the floods which you describe. I have already given the orders to get these programs underway.

The United States, like the Republic of Vietnam, remains devoted to the cause of peace, and our primary purpose is to help your people maintain their independence. If the Communist authorities in North Vietnam will stop their campaign to destroy the Republic of Vietnam, the measures we are taking to assist your defense efforts will no longer be necessary. We shall seek to persuade the Communists to give up their attempts of force and subversion. In any case, we are confident that the Vietnamese people will preserve their independence and gain the peace and prosperity for which they have sought so hard and so long.

Signed: John F. Kennedy

"SUMMARY BIOGRAPHY OF PRESIDENT HO CHI MINH"
(in *Vietnam Courier*, September 8, 1969)

Ho Chi Minh's death on September 3, 1969, at the age of seventy-nine brought to an end fifty years of active political life and marked the close of a revolutionary era in Vietnamese history. The Vietnamese Communist Party (now called the Lao Dong, or Workers' Party) owes its pre-eminent position in North Vietnam today to the strength and stability of its leadership and no man was more instrumental in providing this leadership than Ho Chi Minh.

Born in 1890, he left his native land of central Vietnam at the age of twenty-one to travel abroad. He was leader of the Indochinese Communist Party in the 1930's and returned to Viet-

nam during World War II to lead the liberation movement against French rule. He founded the Viet Minh and brought it to victory over the French. Elected President of the Democratic Republic of Vietnam on September 2, 1945, he held this office for twenty-four years, until his death.

For his countrymen, he personified their heroic and ceaseless struggle for independence from foreign domination.

President Ho Chi Minh (Nguyen Tat Thanh in his childhood and Nguyen Ai Quoc for many years in revolutionary activity later) was born on May 19, 1890, in Kim Lien village, Nam Dan district, Nghe An province, and died on September 3, 1969, in Hanoi.

He was born into a patriotic scholar family of peasant origin and grew up into manhood in a locality with a tradition of heroic resistance to foreign aggression, in a period when the movement for national salvation was seething in Vietnam.

In late 1911, desirous to learn from revolutionary theories and experiences in various foreign countries so as to liberate his homeland from the colonial yoke, President Ho Chi Minh went abroad. He became a worker and took part in the revolutionary mobilization of the peoples in many countries, while militating ceaselessly for the independence and freedom of his own nation. The first Vietnamese to support the great Russian October Revolution and to find in Marxism-Leninism the way to liberate the working class and the peoples in the colonies, he became one of the founders of the French Communist Party at the Tours Congress in 1920. From a genuine patriot, he became an outstanding Communist fighter. "To save one's country and liberate one's nation, there is no other road than that of proletarian revolution," he said.*

* Introduction to Ho Chi Minh, *Selected Writings and Statements*, published in the Soviet Union, 1959.

To combine the struggle of the Vietnamese people with the international workers' movement and the movement for national liberation in the world, he became one of the founding members of the League of the Peoples of French Colonies in 1921, and edited the paper *Le Paria* in France in 1922. In 1923, he was elected to the Executive Committee of the Peasants' International. In 1924, he took part in the Fifth Congress of the Communist International, and was appointed standing member of the Eastern Department, directly in charge of the Southern Section. In 1925, he joined in founding the League of Oppressed Asian Nations, and published two well-known books, *Le Procès de la Colonisation française* (*French Colonization on Trial*) (1925) and *The Path of Revolution* (1927).

To pave the way for a party of Vietnamese Communists, in 1925, he founded the Vietnam Young Revolutionaries' Association in Canton, China, and the "Communist League" as the core for the former, and trained Communist militants to lead the League and introduce Marxism-Leninism into Vietnam. In 1929, the first Communist organizations made their appearance in Vietnam. Empowered by the Executive Committee of the Communist International, he convoked, on February 3, 1930, a "merger conference" to unite various Communist organizations in Vietnam into the Vietnam Communist Party, which later was renamed the Indochinese Communist Party, now the Vietnam Workers' Party. He pointed out at the above-mentioned merger conference that the line for revolution in Vietnam was first to make a national democratic revolution and then to carry out a socialist revolution.

From 1930 to 1940, Comrade Ho Chi Minh continued working in extremely hard and difficult conditions for the liberation of Vietnam and other oppressed nations.

In 1941, he returned to the country, convened the eighth session of the Central Committee of the Indochinese Communist Party to decide the line for the salvation of the country, founded the League for the Independence of Vietnam (Viet Minh), organized the Liberation armed forces, built the base for the revolution, and led the people in local uprisings and in preparing for the general insurrection to seize power in the whole country.

The August (1945) Revolution triumphed, and he proclaimed the Democratic Republic of Vietnam (September 2, 1945). Free general elections were held in the whole country to return a National Assembly, which approved the first democratic constitution of Vietnam. The National Assembly, first legislature, elected him President of the Democratic Republic of Vietnam (1946).

Together with the Central Committee of the Party, President Ho Chi Minh led our entire Party, army, and people to frustrate the schemes of the imperialists, thus preserving and consolidating revolutionary power. Shortly after the August Revolution, the French colonialists staged a comeback to our country. [President Ho Chi Minh] appealed to the entire nation to rise up to defend the independence and freedom of the fatherland and safeguard and develop the gains of the August Revolution. He said, "We would rather sacrifice everything than lose our country or accept slavery." *

At the Second Congress of the Party (1951), he was elected President of the Central Committee of the Party. Under the leadership of the Party's Central Committee headed by President Ho Chi Minh, our people's sacred war of resistance to the French colonialist aggressors achieved success after success and dramatically ended with the great Dien Bien Phu victory (1954).

Following the complete liberation of the North of our country (1954), the Party's Central Committee, and President Ho Chi Minh laid down two strategic tasks for the Vietnamese revolution, that is, to carry out socialist revolution and

* Appeal for nationwide resistance, December 20, 1946.

socialist construction in the North, while striving for the liberation of the South, so as to achieve the reunification of the homeland and complete the national people's democratic revolution in the whole country.

The Third Congress of the Party (1960) charted the line for socialist transformation and socialist construction in the North of our country and that for the national liberation of the South in order to achieve peaceful reunification. The Congress unanimously re-elected Comrade Ho Chi Minh President of the Central Committee of the Vietnam Workers' Party.

Together with the Party's Central Committee, President Ho Chi Minh led our people's great resistance to the war of aggression by the U.S. imperialists. He said, "Our country is one, our nation is one." * and "the South and the North are of the same family. They are brothers of the same blood, nothing can separate them." † "Nothing is more precious than independence and freedom," he emphasized.‡

At the head of the Party's Central Committee, he provided leadership for socialist transformation and socialist revolution in the North of our country. "The North must progress toward socialism, and the most salient feature in the transition period in our country is to advance from a backward agricultural country directly to socialism without going through the stage of capitalist development," he said.§

President Ho Chi Minh always advised us to combine our domestic revolutionary tasks with our international revolutionary obligations. He instructed our entire Party and people to contribute actively to the defense of the socialist system, re-

* Letter to Lawyer Nguyen Huu Tho, President of the Presidium, and the members, of the Central Committee of the South Vietnam National Front for Liberation (June 5, 1967).

† Speech of greeting on the occasion of New Year's Day and the return of the Party's Central Committee and the Government to the capital city (January 1, 1955).

‡ President Ho Chi Minh's appeal (July 17, 1966).

§ "Thirty Years of the Party's Activities."

store unity and identity of mind in our camp and within the international Communist movement on the basis of Marxism-Leninism and proletarian internationalism, and strive to do our bit in the struggle of the world's people for peace, national independence, democracy, and socialism.

President Ho Chi Minh creatively applied Marxism-Leninism to the concrete conditions of our country, mapped our correct lines, took the Vietnamese Revolution from one victory to another. He imaginatively blended the Vietnamese nation's finest traditions with the thorough-going revolutionary thoughts of the working class and with Marxist-Leninist ideology, and closely combined genuine patriotism with proletarian internationalism. The revolutionary cause of our Party and President Ho Chi Minh has ushered in a new era in the history of the Vietnamese nation, an era in which the Vietnamese people defeat various imperialist forces, liberate the nation, and achieve people's democracy and build socialism in their country.

He strongly believed in the great force of the masses and devoted all his life to the Revolution, the people, and the fatherland. He was a bright and perfect impersonation of collective spirit, sense of organization, and revolutionary virtues: loyalty to the Party, dedication to the Party, dedication to the people, industry, thrift, honesty and integrity, public-mindedness and selflessness, modesty and simplicity.

President Ho Chi Minh's cause is truly great. He was the founding father of the Marxist-Leninist Party of Vietnam, the Vietnam people's united front, the Vietnam people's armed forces, and the Democratic Republic of Vietnam, and credited with a great contribution to the strengthening of international solidarity.

President Ho Chi Minh was the great teacher of the Vietnamese revolution, the beloved leader of the working class and entire nation of Vietnam, an outstanding fighter, a gifted activist in the international Communist movement and the national liberation movement. His name will live forever in the heart of every patriotic Vietnamese, and his cause will certainly be carried forward victoriously.

"POLITICAL TESTAMENT," BY *Ho Chi Minh*

Following is the full text of the will of President Ho Chi Minh, read by Le Duan, First Secretary of the Central Committee of the Vietnam Workers' Party, at a solemn ceremony in Hanoi in memory of the late President of the Democratic Republic of Vietnam, on September 9, 1969. In this "political testament," he bids farewell to his people and urges the Party to contribute to the healing of the Sino-Soviet split.

Will of President Ho Chi Minh:

In the patriotic struggle against U.S. aggression, we shall have indeed to undergo more difficulties and sacrifices, but we are sure to win total victory.

This is an absolute certainty.

It is my intention, when that day comes, to make a tour of both North and South to congratulate our heroic compatriots, cadres, and combatants, to pay visits to our old people, our beloved youths and children.

Then, on behalf of our people, I will go to the fraternal countries of the socialist camp and friendly countries in the whole world, and thank them for their wholehearted support and assistance to our people's patriotic struggle against U.S. aggression.

Tu Fu, the well-known Chinese poet of the Tang epoch,

wrote: "In all times, few are those who reach the age of seventy."

This year, with my seventy-nine years, I am among those few people; still, my mind is lucid, though my health has somewhat weakened in comparison with previous years. When one is beyond seventy, health deteriorates with age. This is no wonder.

But who can forecast for how long I can continue to serve the revolution, the fatherland, and the people?

That is the reason why I leave these few lines in anticipation of the day when I go and join venerable Karl Marx, Lenin, and other revolutionary elders; in this way, our compatriots in the whole country, the comrades in the Party, and our friends in the world will not be surprised.

First, I will speak about the Party: Thanks to its close unity and total dedication to the working class, the people, and the fatherland, our Party has been able, since its founding, to unite, organize, and lead our people in an ardent struggle, and advance them from victory to victory.

Unity is an extremely precious tradition of our Party and people. All comrades, from the Central Committee down to the cell, must preserve the union and unity of mind in the Party as the apple of their eyes.

Within the Party, to achieve broad democracy and to practice self-criticism and criticism regularly and seriously is the best way to consolidate and develop the union and unity of mind in the Party. Genuine affection should prevail among all comrades.

Ours is a Party in power; each Party member, each cadre must be deeply imbued with revolutionary morality, and show industry, thrift, integrity, uprightness, total dedication to the public cause, exemplary selflessness. Our Party should preserve its entire purity; it should remain worthy of its role as the leader and a very loyal servant of the people.

The Working Youth Union members and our young people

as a whole are of excellent nature, eager to volunteer for vanguard tasks, undeterred by difficulties, and striving for progress. The Party must give much attention to their education in revolutionary morality and train them into successors of the building of socialism.

Training and educating the revolutionary generation to come is a highly important and necessary task.

Our laboring people, both in the plains and in the mountain areas, have for ages suffered hardships, feudal and colonial oppression, and exploitation. Furthermore, they have experienced many years of war.

Yet our people have shown great heroism, great courage, ardent enthusiasm, and are very hard-working. They have always followed the Party since it came into being, and they have always been loyal to it.

The Party must work out a good plan for economic and cultural development with a view to ceaselessly raising the living standard of the people.

The resistance war against U.S. aggression may drag out. Our compatriots may have to undergo new sacrifices in terms of property and human lives. In any case, we must be resolved to fight against the U.S. aggressors till final victory.

Our rivers, our mountains, our men will always remain. When the Yanks are defeated, we will build our country to be ten times more beautiful.

No matter what difficulties and hardships may lie ahead, our people are sure to win total victory. The U.S. imperialists will have to pull out. Our fatherland will be reunified. Our compatriots in the North and in the South will be reunited under the same roof. Our country will have the final honor of being a small nation which, through a heroic struggle, has defeated two big imperialists—France and America—and made a worthy contribution to the National Liberation Movement.

About the world Communist movement: Having dedicated

my whole life to the cause of the revolution, the more I am proud to see the growth of the international Communist and workers' movement, the more deeply I am grieved at the dissensions that are dividing the fraternal parties.

I wish that our Party will do its best to contribute effectively to the restoration of unity among the fraternal parties on the basis of Marxism-Leninism and prolitarian internationalism, in a way consonant to the requirements of heart and reason.

I am sure that the fraternal parties and countries will unite again.

About personal matters: In all my life, I have wholeheartedly and with all my forces, served the fatherland, the Revolution, and the people. Now if I should depart from this world, there is nothing that I am sorry to have done. I regret only not being able to serve longer and more.

After my passing away, great funerals should be avoided in order not to waste the time and money of the people.

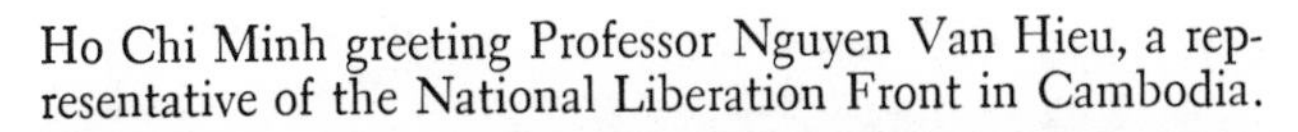
Ho Chi Minh greeting Professor Nguyen Van Hieu, a representative of the National Liberation Front in Cambodia.

Finally, to the whole people, the whole Party, the whole army, to my nephews and nieces, youths and children, I leave behind my boundless affection.

I also convey my fraternal greetings to the comrades, friends, youths, and children in the world.

My ultimate wish is that our whole Party and people, closely united in the struggle, build a peaceful, unified, independent, democratic, and prosperous Vietnam, and make a worthy contribution to the world revolution.

SPEECH TO LOCAL OFFICIALS, BY *President Nguyen Van Thieu* (April 12, 1969)

A career army officer, General Nguyen Van Thieu was elected President of South Vietnam on September, 1968, after serving more than one year as chief of the executive. On April 12, 1969, President Thieu addressed a graduation class for village and hamlet chiefs. His informal speech is tailored to an audience of rural officials, on whom Thieu relies to enforce the anti-Communist policies of the Saigon government in the countryside. The speech also throws some light on the little-known personality of Thieu himself. He was born some forty-six years ago in a modest family of small landowners in central Vietnam. His father was the village chief.

One of my objectives is social reform. Our society is poor, miserable, and filled with injustices. I am not a townsman; I stayed in my native village until I completed my high

An old woman follows the old ways, pounding her paddy in a stone vessel. (Today, most farmers bring their rice to automatic mills to be husked and polished.) This woman's teeth are lacquered black, an ancient practice that younger women have abandoned.

school studies. In 1945, when the Vietnamese Communists seized power, I was a village chief, and then a district chief. I will talk to you about this later. For this reason, I understand village affairs well.

My family was poor, possessing only five hectares of rice fields. I know what problems my village has and to what extent the population has been oppressed and has suffered. So, in my opinion, social reform—I tell you the truth—does not consist in building beautiful houses and buildings for townspeople's enjoyment. Some day, if you have time to visit Independence Palace, you will see that the International Guest

Hall, the Conference Hall, and the Credentials Room are very beautiful and are the pride of our country. But my bedroom cannot surely equal that of a contractor or a doctor or an American colonel. What are my meals? I eat only things I like, and not exquisite meals.

Therefore, I know for certain these matters. I was a farmer; in my childhood, I went to see reaping and irrigation ditches dug. Since my village was a fishing village, I know about fish and can talk with you about fishing. Therefore, I know problems in villages and hamlets. Although I am President, my relatives are still living in the countryside and, barefoot and clad in black pyjamas, they work in the field like other peasants instead of being brought into Independence Palace and appointed to important posts.

I know my relatives' problems in the countryside. When speaking of social reform in the villages and hamlets, I mean avoiding injustice, eliminating people-bullying tyrants and despots, and preventing the abuse of authority, arrogance, and oppression. To carry out social reform in villages and hamlets is to make people happier, to act so that each person will become a small landowner and each worker will eventually have some shares in enterprises so that he can buy medicine for his sick children. If they do not have money to buy medicine, the government must, at least, help them. If they cannot afford to send their expectant wives to private hospitals, they may send their wives to the district or provincial maternity clinics. Their children will be able to obtain an elementary education or, if possible, a secondary education. The government certainly cannot give them everything, but will give them part of what they need. This is social reform.

I am very simple. I do not talk big. I do not want to tell lies. I do not promise when you gentlemen will have buildings or storied houses. No. Just live in thatched houses, with the condition that you will have medicine to take when you are ill; your children can go to school; you can meet your daily needs. You possess small radios over which you can follow classical theatrical performances at your leisure; you can go to the provincial capital once every few months; and, on holidays or during the Tet holidays, you can buy some flowers, some pictures, to decorate your home. I am sure that many people in our society still lack these simple things. If everyone acquired just these things, he would be happy enough. These things would provide a basis for gradual improvement. As I have told you, our nation is a mature nation, our people are a developed, self-reliant people. Our nation is, excuse me for saying, like a child walking, running, and working. It is, excuse me for saying so, like a tree, a bamboo shoot, a small or big bamboo tree. We must not be in too big a hurry but should proceed from a firm basis. I am determined to build this basis, as long as the people maintain their confidence in me so that I can stay on.

Fruit-sellers wait for customers in front of the Eden, a leading movie house in Saigon. Only a small percentage of the Vietnamese speak French today, but movies are still dubbed in French, with subtitles in Vietnamese, English, or Chinese.

THE WAR AND ITS POLITICAL REPERCUSSIONS

"SOUTH VIETNAM: A CASCADE OF GOVERNMENTS," BY *François Sully*

Following is a bare outline of the changes in government that have taken place in Saigon since 1954. These do not include brief coups d'état *without issue, or prolonged periods of domestic crisis that did not topple a government.*

As a result of the Geneva agreement on the cessation of hostilities in Vietnam signed on July 20, 1954, Vietnam was divided at the Seventeenth Parallel. South of the demarcation line, a republican form of government was chosen by national referendum, while the territory north of the Seventeenth Parallel adopted a Communist regime.

From 1956 to 1963, South Vietnam was governed under a constitution that provided for a strong executive, a unicameral assembly, and a judicial system. Ngo Dinh Diem was elected president in October, 1955, and re-elected in April, 1961. As a result of intensified insurgency, President Diem declared a state of emergency on October 18 and assumed the power to rule by decree. On November 1, 1963, he was overthrown in a *coup d'état*, and the constitution of 1956 was abrogated.

"Provisional Charter No. 1," dated November 4, 1963, provided that Vietnam remain a republic, with legislative and executive powers centralized in a Military Revolutionary Council headed by General Duong Van Minh, pending adoption of a new constitution. On November 6, a provisional cabinet was installed in office under Premier Nguyen Ngoc Tho; the cabinet contained both civilians and military men and had been approved by the military leaders.

On January 30, 1964, General Nguyen Khanh replaced General Duong Van Minh as chairman of the Military Revolutionary Council, following a military coup. On February 8, Premier Tho resigned and General Nguyen Khanh was installed as premier of a new Vietnamese government. On August 16, Khanh was elected Vietnamese president by the Military Revolutionary Council and installed a new constitution. On August 27, the constitution was withdrawn. Coups and countercoups for and against General Khanh continued during September.

On October 26, the Military Revolutionary Council elected Phan Khac Suu, a widely respected elder statesman, as chief of state, in a return to civilian government. On November 1, Tran Van Huong was named premier. The new government consummated the restoration of civilian control by the appointment of a High National Council to act as a temporary legislative body. However, on December 20, 1964, the Armed Forces Council abolished the High National Council and, in the face of mounting opposition to the new government, asked Premier Huong to resign on January 27, 1965.

Following an unsuccessful attempt by General Khanh to regain control of the government, Dr. Phan Huy Quat, a former minister of foreign affairs, organized a new government and assumed office on February 16, 1965. Mr. Suu continued as chief of state, and a National Legislative Council was established to act as Vietnam's legislature.

In June, 1965, Dr. Quat and Mr. Suu resigned, and General Nguyen Cao Ky became premier of a military government with civilian participation.

The sovereignty of South Vietnam was provisionally vested in the Congress of the Armed Forces. Subordinate to the Congress was the Directorate, which was entrusted with the exercise of power and director of governmental affairs. The chairman of the Directorate, General Nguyen Van Thieu, was in effect chief of state.

On April 1, 1967, Chief of State Nguyen Van Thieu promulgated a democratic constitution voted by the Constituent Assembly on March 18. It provides for a modified presidential system, a bicameral legislature, an independent judiciary, and a basic bill of rights for all citizens.

On September 1, 1967, a presidential election was held and generals Nguyen Van Thieu and Nguyen Cao Ky were elected president and vice president respectively.

"TOWARD A POLITICAL REVITALIZATION," BY *Tran Thi Lan* (in *Saigon Daily News*, July 3, 1968)

Since 1954, the government of South Vietnam has been struggling to maintain its political viability in the face of overwhelming obstacles, including, at present, a full-scale war fought with much ferocity the length and breadth of its territory. We have seen in a previous article the lack of political stability prevailing in the South. Another problem, eloquently stated in this article, is the absence of political vitality and the failure of a military-dominated government to permit a genuine opposition.

This country's political life has remained disorganized and sterile for decades. There are many obstacles to the blossoming of healthy, fruitful political activities. A major stumbling block is the government's reluctance to tolerate nonconformity.

President Nguyen Van Thieu told the political congress at Independence Palace that he was prepared to accept an opposition. When asked to comment on this statement, most politicians present at the meeting expressed their doubt that Thieu could be taken at his word. This shows how much the people in power are held in distrust by the country's politicians.

This situation is quite understandable. No government here has shown its willingness to promote political life. Most often, the very politicians who used to be active as politicians became uncompromising when they got into the government.

Vietnam, of course, could not have a free political life under the Chinese imperialists or the French colonialists, simply because they did not tolerate dissidence and independence of mind. The country's political activities, therefore, had to be shrouded in secrecy, which naturally entailed a multiplicity of political organizations, mutual suspicions among the various groups, the fluidity of political goals, and especially the lack of widespread popular support for most politicians.

The Diem regime was not favorable to a healthy political life either. It did not tolerate independent political parties, which had to go underground. It persecuted nonconformist politicians. To keep up a façade of democracy, former President Diem allowed a few political organizations to operate, but it was clear to all that such organizations were only his tools. The National Revolutionary Movement (*Phong Trao Cach Mang Quoc Gia*), for instance, was merely a slogan-shouting outfit whose sole activity was to sing praises of the authoritarian regime.

Strongmen

The successive military regimes following the overthrow of Diem were even worse as far as normal political life is concerned. Former strongman General Nguyen Khanh, for instance, did not hesitate to declare that "the armed forces is the father of the nation" and professed utter disdain for politicians whom he uniformly called "rice-and-meat" politicians (*chinh khach xoi thit*). The terminology coined by him has remained notorious ever since.

The Thieu-Ky regime followed virtually the same pattern of Gaullist disdain for politicians. While dozens of political groups were formed under this regime, none was allowed to operate decently.

The election of Thieu and Ky as president and vice president, respectively, has been rather a legal confirmation of their power only. The incipient front of opposition, which was headed by Phan Khac Suu and had the participation of most unsuccessful presidential and senatorial candidates, could never get off the ground because its more articulate members were harassed by the newly-elected regime. A number of nonconformist politicians and religious leaders were taken into "protective custody" without a plausible explanation. The first cabinet failed to include politicians, and the second one still basically included apolitical technocrats.

The situation, understandably, has degenerated into a state of deep mistrust toward all people in authority. Thieu's act of confidence in convening the political congress last Saturday, while meritorious, is only a tiny step toward allaying people's fears. He has to follow up his initiative with bold and consistent gestures if he wants to convince the population, especially politicians, of his sincerity.

No Press Freedom

While no one expects to have complete freedom of the press in time of war, every one, including journalists, must be given a due process of law and a chance to defend himself and plead his cause. The practice of suspending a newspaper arbitrarily or harassing journalists must be stopped once and for all.

To bring about an atmosphere of political détente necessary to colorful and fruitful political activities, the government must also solve the problem of political opponents immediately and with open-mindedness. The political arrests and trials in the past few years must be revised. Innocent detainees must be set free, while guilty ones must be given a fair process of law.

The government must also allow the exiled generals to come home if they so wish. Should there be plausible reasons against their return, as Premier Huong once intimated, the

Sampans in the Bay of Ha Long, North Vietnam

government had better spell out such reasons in all candor instead of resorting to vague argument as it has done so far.

President Thieu has promised to give material assistance to political parties; including the opposition. This is an excellent idea, although it is still difficult to convince people that in helping politicians the government is not trying to "buy" them. I believe, however, that if Thieu continues to hold out his hand, it would not take politicians too long to respond favorably.

The real problem of political activity, of course, is not lack of material facilities. It is the gnawing doubt that the government is sincere this time. If, on the one hand, Thieu urges politicians to operate actively, and on the other hand, he continues to adhere to political dogmatism and rely on a restricted circle of trusted followers, the atmosphere will be no more favorable to a political revitalization than it has been in the past.

"WHY NORTH AND SOUTH VIETNAM SHOULD BE REUNITED," BY *Tran Xuan Ly* (unpublished, Saigon, 1969)

The partition of Vietnam into two countries with vastly different political regimes—a socialist state in the North, a military-dominated regime in the South—has been, since 1954, a fact of life. How much the Vietnamese would like to end this abnormal division of their nation and rebuild its unity seems difficult to adjust with the seemingly irreconciliable characters of the two political societies now centered on Hanoi and Saigon. Unless one of them would willingly or forcibly forfeit its own distinctive way of life, it is difficult to visualize how the dream of one Vietnam united from the border of China to the tip of the Camau Peninsula could be made real. In the second part of the twentieth century, ideologies and the harsh necessities of balancing political and military power along well-defined geographic lines have be-

come stronger realities than the emotional bonds surviving within the members of a divided nation. This article presents an emotional case for reunification.

Despite regional differences between Northerners and Southerners, the two Vietnams are still culturally and emotionally one nation. In fact, the 1954 Geneva agreements did not create two sovereign nations and the partition between North and South—a necessity for the regroupment of French troops to the South after Dien Bien Phu—was never meant to be permanent. Vietnam, since then, is a nation with its

Sampans on a canal at Rach Gia, South Vietnam

head in Hanoi, its heart in the old imperial city of Hue, and its breadbasket in the fertile Mekong Delta.

At best, a return to the 1954 agreements and to the formula of two Vietnams can be a transitory solution bringing a temporary peace. For it will ignore two basic facts. One is that elections in Vietnam, instead of solving problems, tend to create new ones. The second is that the case for reunification is stronger than foreign observers may think. After all, some 400,000 Southern guerrillas have died since 1960, because they believed in reunification. The hard truth is that there is no such entity as two Vietnams; there are almost as many Southerners in the Hanoi Government as Northerners in the present Saigon administration. Mai Van Bo, the senior Hanoi diplomat in Paris, is a former schoolmate of Pham Dang Lam, the ambassador from Saigon. Both are from the same Mekong Delta province. Ton Duc Thang, Hanoi's vice president, is a Southerner. And, of course, General Nguyen Cao Ky, our maverick soldier-politician in Saigon, is a Northerner.

One major reason favoring reunification is that North and South Vietnam are so economically interdependent that neither can hope for a bright future if free access to the other's resources is denied to him. South Vietnam has always been the ricebowl of Vietnam, while North Vietnam, with its rich mineral resources, has the potential for industrialization. If reunification cannot be achieved, the South will continue for an indefinite period to be the economic ward of the United States, while the North—like Cuba—will be kept alive with massive transfusion of Sino-Soviet assistance. But sooner or later, the natural forces for unification will manifest themselves.

The emotional attachment to a unified Vietnam is so true that the constitutions of both North and South Vietnam stress that *Vietnam is a united and indivisible nation extending from the Chinese border to the tip of the Camau peninsula.* In the 1967 presidential elections, the symbol of the

Thieu-Ky ticket was a map of a unified Vietnam. General Duong Van Minh once wrote in *Foreign Affairs* that South and North Vietnamese "should live under the same roof and in freedom." No government ignoring the reunification question can convince the majority of Vietnamese that they have a government they can trust. And this single fact, perhaps, explains all the difficulties met by South Vietnamese leaders since the fateful decision to ignore their *de facto* commitment to general elections in July, 1956. One of President Ho Chi Minh's dreams, before he faded into history, was to realize the unity of the Vietnamese nation.

Stretched-out Reunification

Undoubtedly, the advocates of a perpetual partition of Vietnam along the German model will make their voice heard, for simplistic solutions have always strong appeal on those ignoring the intricate complexities of the Asian drama. Partition could work, but only for a very limited number of years, providing that trade and other normal relations are resumed after a ceasefire. Even Ho Chi Minh, whose socialist revolution is trying to fulfill the Vietnamese dream for political unification, was aware of the problem's complexity and was not pressing for "immediate" reunification. Ten years, perhaps, would have satisfied him. Living under Western influences for nearly a century, many South Vietnamese have developed a different way of life than that of their Northern brothers. Obviously, some arrangement respecting the "regional rights" of the South Vietnamese will have to be nailed down. Even when living under one roof, members of the same family do not necessarily share the same tastes.

"CAN SOUTH VIETNAM SURVIVE DEMOCRACY?," BY *Nguyen Ngoc Rao* (in *Saigon Daily News*, July 10, 1968)

"A democracy without a National Assembly is unconceivable. But our democracy can hardly afford the luxury of a National Assembly at present," said a South Vietnamese senator.

The amorphous nature and sluggish performance of this first National Assembly of the second republic seem to substantiate the senator's remarks. However, most South Vietnamese who are loyal to the government take pride in the existence of this democratic institution and would feel unhappy without it.

This is a bicameral Assembly. The Senate, commonly called Upper House, has sixty members selected by a national electorate in joint lists of ten candidates each.

Elected under this system, the senators are believed to be fairly well known to the population and to have broad views on the country's problems. Most belong to the upper classes—lawyers, doctors, retired generals, and businessmen. Their average age is forty-five.

The 137 members of the House of Representatives, or Lower House, on the contrary, were elected individually and in constituencies. They are supposed to be aware of the aspirations and needs of the population in their areas.

Most are retired civil servants or junior military officers, teachers, small businessmen, and "notables." Their average age is thirty-eight.

The constitution gives more legislative power to the House than to the Senate. All drafts of bills, which the President, Senators, and Deputies can introduce, must be submitted first to the Lower House for debate. If the House refuses to debate on it, a bill has no chance to become law.

Once a bill has been passed by the House, it must go to the Senate for review and endorsement. If the Senate agrees with the House, the bill is sent to the President for promulgation.

But if the Senate disagrees, it has to send the bill back to the house for consideration. The Senate's recommendations can be overriden by the House if it can muster a two-thirds majority vote.

The President can propose amendments to a bill sent to him. But the Assembly can reject his requests with a vote of more than one-half of the Senators and Deputies.

Besides legislative, the Assembly has other prerogatives. It can ratify treaties and international agreements, make decisions on declaring war or holding peace talks, control the government in the carrying out of the national policy, recommend replacement of part or all of the Cabinet, question government officials from the Premier on down, investigate government performance, approve the appointments of chiefs of diplomatic missions as well as of rectors of the universities, nominate the justices to the Supreme Court, and even remove from office the President or Vice President of the republic.

A senator's term of office is six years. One-half of the Senate is up for re-election every three years. Representatives serve four years.

Although the current South Vietnamese National Assembly still seems a long way from maturity, it is commonly considered the pride of this fledgling democracy.

"EAST MEETS WEST IN THE PX," BY *Raymond A. Sokolov* (in *Newsweek*, July 29, 1968)

"For example, in the bus pool, Supervisor-in-Chief Ben, with his 'brown nose,' factblinded Staff Sergeant E-6

Martino to get a cut from the stolen stuff. Every time a cheating or stealing driver was turned in to Ben, Ben patted him on the back and said, 'They want to get you fired but I'll do my best to help you out.' That meant a bottle of whisky or a carton of cigarettes right there. I'll tell you, boys, that goddam Ben got more American commodities in his house than the Brink PX got. He'd bought three new houses since Martino's assignment."

This purports to be part of an American Pfc.'s message to his father back home about the way it is in Saigon. It is, in fact, the literary creation of H. T. (Huynh Thanh) Tam, a 32-year-old Saigonese who has spent the last ten years as an interpreter with the U.S. Special Forces in Vietnam. A school dropout who "always got bad marks in Vietnamese and English," Tam "learned to speak English well just sitting around swapping jokes and war stories" with the Green Berets. He also read cast-off American detective novels by the pile. "That's where I guess I picked up my writing style," he says. "I don't really remember when I started writing, but it was at a time when I felt I'd read enough books and I thought I could write one." And write he did.

Shortly after the Tet offensive, working "sixteen to eighteen hours a day," Tam polished off seven stories, or, as he calls them, "motive-packed features from a multifaceted war." He writes his stories in English ("I'd make more mistakes in Vietnamese. Call me a literary misfit if you want to") in a tiny Saigon flat that reeks of *nuoc mam*, a pungent, typically Vietnamese fish sauce, and then gives them to his friend Alex (Marty) Martinez, a mechanic with the U.S. contracting firm Pacific Architects and Engineers. Marty, who "cleans up" Tam's grammar, also put up the money to publish *Saigon 7* at a local job-printing house, which ran off 5,000 copies at 12 cents apiece on cheap paper, with a type face left over from the days of French hegemony.

So far, Tam and Martinez have sold 1,000 copies on the local market. U.S. official red tape bars them from regular GI newsstands, though the original idea behind the book was to reach the vast reading public of American enlisted men, "in a language they understand best." "I try to get inside the mind of a soldier," Tam remarked last week, undaunted by a foot-deep flood of water in the lobby of his building, "and I try to describe about war and the emotions that go with it just the way he would do if he were writing."

Though readers back in CONUS (Continental U.S.) may be inclined to "laugh a big mouth" at this enterprise and dismiss it as barbarically written pulp, Tam's stories reveal much more than the best straightforward accounts what happens when we really do win the hearts and minds of the Vietnamese.

Tam has learned his lessons from the "hairless, Buddha-like" Americans well. The first step is self-hate. He has one of his characters say to an American officer: "Sir, we cannot control our people. That's why you Americans are here to help." Totally convinced that the war is saving his people from slavery under "Honcho Chi," he does allow himself the luxury of occasionally criticizing the American presence, constructively for the most part, the way a GI might to a Viet pal. But his real loyalty is to the culture of America, the American way where "everything is permissible . . . as long as it brings in money to everyone," where "Johnny Carson was making his million a year." Tam's Vietnam festers with strange, distorted echoes of America. In his Saigon, a Viet man admires a Viet woman because she has "Liz Taylor's kind of fat." Sixteen-year-old whores wear their hair like the Supremes, and at a civilian party an all-girl rock group with electric guitars plays "I Left My Heart in San Francisco."

Tam's Saigon is also a nightmare of red tape, inflation, revolting poverty, and dislocation. Of this he offers frequent glimpses in language that is affecting and weirdly poetic: "Paddyfield worker all day and house servant at night, she had gone away with the TB that'd been bigger than her lungs." And then there are scenes like this, culturally corrupt and surreal: "Darkness was pulling down, fading another day away. What a man should have done now was sit at a TV side, his hands on the supersensitive surfaces of a body molded to him like sweet plastic."

"No country," Tam writes, "is Alice Wonderland, especially when there is live fire in it." But his stories give devastating proof that the war is hardly more destructive than the half-baked cultural invasion it has brought with it across the Pacific. "East is East and West is West," says this Kipling in reverse, "the difference is as large as a distance halfway around the world." Sadly, the twain are meeting.

"IN A HAMLET CLOSE TO SAIGON," BY *An Anonymous Writer of the Liberation Front* (in *Vietnam Courier,* October 5, 1968)

In glowing terms, a member of the National Liberation Front (NLF) underground relates the creation of a guerrilla unit in Ap Giong, a small hamlet in Long An Province along the Vam Co Dong River, some twenty-five miles southwest of Saigon. As protection against government observation planes, the scenes he describes took place at night "under the eerie glare of flares dropped by American planes."

Destroy the Road

At dusk the noise had begun: bamboo tocsins, tin cans, empty napalm containers . . . resounded over the vast sugar-cane fields, mingled with the hubbub of people calling, running, and shouting through megaphones. If a man would stand still and listen, he would be able to get an idea of the bustle going on in Ap Giong and the ebullient revolutionary atmosphere prevailing there. An enemy military post stood less than half a kilometer away; yet the megaphones went right on urging the people to the places where bonfires were tearing off to shreds the darkness along highways 8 and 10. There, since nightfall, the people of Ap Giong, bringing along balls of cooked rice, bamboo baskets, picks and shovels, dynamite charges, and bomb duds, had set to destroy enemy communications. Each bonfire marked a stretch of road being cut to pieces. At dusk, a few rifle shots had been heard, but this did not last very long. A megaphone recounted what had happened: The rounds had been fired by a platoon of puppet soldiers headed by a man named Nhi. But Nhi's wife was among the road-destroyers. Without a word, she stepped out, came right up to Nhi and stood defiantly with arms akimbo facing her husband's gun muzzle. Nhi eventually gave way and soon another bonfire was lit.

Walking along the road, I remembered the fierce resistance put up by the Ap Giong people in 1958 to protect their cane fields against enemy destruction. Now, as then, the fields stretched out in immense expanses, dotted with bomb craters. Through the cuts made in the banks of the canals, flowed water from the Vam Co River. There I saw flickering kerosene lights and heard the noise of machetes working on hard wood. Some people were coughing, apparently old folks. Coming closer, I saw white goatees and wrinkled foreheads, and the sight moved me to tears. Elderly men and women were building bridges across canals and cuts in the roads, for their

Farmers in Central Vietnam flee their village to escape fighting. In the background loom the Annamite Mountains.

"sons" in the Liberation Army to move more quickly in the direction of Saigon. Spreading rice husks on the mud to make the paths less slippery and throwing bridges across road gaps and canals, such was the kind of job devolved upon the "white-haired-army". Old people were crowding in to volunteer for revolutionary jobs, and so an "office" had to be set up to distribute tasks. An elderly woman who was floundering in the water trying to put up a pillar for a bridge said to another, "It took me a great deal of talking to convince Ut, the Front secretary, that I am perfectly fit for work. Ah, how lucky the young people are! They don't have to beg for assignments! They are given guns and plenty of opportunities to fight!"

Arm the Women

That night, before the attack on the enemy sector of Hau Nghia, I took a stroll along the canals, crossed the newly-built bridges, heading in the direction of Saigon. The flares in the sky over the city had become even denser. Enemy artillery was firing on the outskirts. Three hundred shells fell on the territory of Ap Giong: its "share of fire." But there were nonetheless crowds of people in the fields. Amid the roar of guns, people were arguing impassionedly. About 100 had volunteered to join the reinforcements for Saigon, but more were asking to go. A quota of 200 had been reserved for Ap Giong and Duc Hoa people wishing to enlist in the district armed forces, but this was far from enough. Whoever was given a gun jumped for joy, but others loudly protested that they were every bit as good. The military cadre of Ap Giong talked himself hoarse calling on people to "be reasonable, fair-minded, and display class solidarity." Everybody nodded vigorous approval, but this didn't stop the disputes and scuffles over who should get the guns first. . . . Sister Toi was among the first to be issued a rifle, for her husband had recently been killed by the enemy. Uncle Ton said he should be made a member of a 82-mm. mortar crew, for an enemy shell from Hau Nghia had knocked down his cattle shed. Uncle Tu Dia had to yield his submachine gun to Sister Lam, for his wife had just given birth to a child and he had to stay home to look after her. The patch of field where the weapons were being distributed was like a boiling pot, where everything was in effervescence. People came and went, talked, discussed. Men who had just been handed weapons strutted about, humming folksongs, then abruptly switching to a march. Others boasted about a bumper crop of beans or of sugar cane, or talked about the high price he had got for his poultry at the market.

But now the sound of gunfire had burst all around. The people of Ap Giong, whether belonging to a military formation or not, stood ready for combat. Flares were drifting over Saigon. On the ground the flames of the people's struggle were consuming the enemy. The sound of drums and tocsins was calling on the people of Ap Giong to surge up and join the hurricane that was sweeping the aggressors away.

"BUILDING UP ARMED FORCES," BY *Truong Chinh* (in *The Resistance Will Win* [Hanoi, 1966])

This book was written by Truong Chinh, the leading Marxist theoretician of Vietnam, in 1947, at a time when the Vietnamese were waging war against the French. The chapter reproduced below was written later and added to the third edition. In the book, Truong Chinh explains the strategy of waging a people's war of resistance, a long-term struggle based on guerrilla warfare.

To win the war, a powerful armed force is needed. At this initial stage of the resistance, we have two categories of armed forces: the regular army and the popular forces, the latter being made up of the guerrillas and the self-defense militia. But in the near future, these forces will probably comprise three categories: regular army, regional guerrillas, and self-defense militia. . . .

The people are the reserve of the armed forces in general, the self-defense militia is the reserve of the regional troops, and the latter constitute the reserve of the regular army. This conforms to the law of development of people's war and the people's army, for these originate from the people. They progress and become ever more important in size and strength, and richer in forms.

Ours is a revolutionary army of the people, fighting for the people.

The goal for which it fights is closely linked with the revolutionary task at each stage of the Vietnamese revolution. And as at present our revolution is a people's national democratic one, its immediate goal is national independence and new-type democracy. . . .

Our army belongs to the people, chiefly the workers and peasants led by the working class. Its members are workers, peasants, and revolutionary intellectuals, the workers and especially the peasants comprising the overwhelming majority. Generally speaking, the officers must stem from the basic strata and adhere to Marxism-Leninism.

Political work in the army plays a decisive role as regards its build-up as well as its fighting capacity. It aims at inculcating in the army ardent patriotism, true proletarian internationalism, high combativeness, sacrifice for the nation's lofty interests, absolute loyalty to the fatherland and the people, self-conscious discipline, constant concern about inner unity, solidarity with the people, and ability to undermine the enemy's morale.

The standpoint and thinking of the officers and men must be constantly consolidated and their revolutionary virtues fostered. Concurrently, their basic knowledge in strategy and tactics must be cultivated along a correct line. To this end, particular attention should be paid to their education in Marxism-Leninism and to their grasping the line and policies of the leading organizations and government. The cadres in general, and the officers in particular, must study Marxist-Leninist military classics and "On Protracted War" by Comrade Mao Tse-tung. They must become well acquainted with the military writings of our predecessors, such as "Essentials on Military Art" and "Proclamation to the Army," by Tran Hung Dao, "Report on the Victory over the Mings" and "Selection of Orders to the Army," by Nguyen Trai, and so on.

As for unity with the people, the army must be well aware that the people are the water and the army is like fish living in it. Therefore, it must ceaselessly improve its relations with the people, whose constant aid is most needed to defeat the enemy. To strengthen this unity, the army men must do political work among the population and help them in production, liquidation of illiteracy, organization of prophylactic hygiene, and military and guerrilla warfare training. Moreover, they must help the population realize their task, which is to support the army in all respects and by every possible means, so that the latter may have all the necessary conditions to defeat the aggressors. As a matter of course, this support must be in line with the policies of the leading organization and the government.

"THE PEOPLE OF THE ENTIRE COUNTRY ARE OF ONE MIND IN STEPPING UP THE GREAT PATRIOTIC WAR," BY *General Vo Nguyen Giap* (1966)

The war against the Americans began in earnest for the National Liberation Front (NLF) and its allies in 1965, with the introduction of large-scale American ground troops and massive amounts of material. This changed the tempo of fighting and caused military leaders in Hanoi to re-evaluate their tactics and strategy. In this article, the North Vietnamese Commander in Chief, Vo Nguyen Giap, who has led the DRV army since 1944 and brought it to victory against France, examines the new situation. He carefully delineates the reasons why the Americans cannot win the war.

The dispatch of an expeditionary corps for direct invasion of our country is itself subject to weaknesses so fundamental that they cannot surmount them.

First, the more troops the U.S. imperialists bring in to invade our country, the clearer they expose their faces as aggressors and their lackeys as country-sellers, thus making the contradiction between the American imperialists and our nation ever sharper and fiercer. . . .

Second, the U.S. imperialists deploy their troops to invade our country at a time when the strategy of their "special war" has basically gone bankrupt. . . . Though they may bring in hundreds of thousands of troops, they still cannot avoid being driven into a defensive strategic position which compels them to scatter their forces for defense as well as offense, thereby making it hard for them to regain the initiative they long for.

Third, due to the unjust character of its war, the U.S. expeditionary corps is fighting without an ideal and hence has low morale. On the southern battlefield, it has to cope with a people's war; the strategy and tactics based on their bourgeois military outlook are of no use. The organization, composition, and training of the American Army in general are not fit to tackle our entire people's revolutionary war; it does not take into account the great difficulties encountered in a strange terrain and climate, and the considerable demands in the fields of supply and logistics.

Fourth, the purpose of the U.S. imperialists' introduction of troops into the South is to prevent the collapse of the puppet army and administration and to create new conditions for the consolidating and strengthening of their puppet forces; the U.S. imperialists, however, directly invade the southern part of our country at a moment when the puppet army and administration are seriously decaying. In such a situation, the more active the U.S. aggression is, the more isolated and divided the puppet army and administration will become, and the greater the contradictions between the U.S. imperialists and their henchmen will grow; thus, those who are in the ranks of the puppet army and administration but still have some national feeling will become more conscious and return to the people's side in greater numbers. Consequently, as the U.S. imperialists build up their military forces, not only will they be unable to retrieve the predicament of the puppet army and administration, but they will also accelerate the latter's collapse and annihilation. . . .

Fifth, having started the war in the South, the U.S. imperialists are being condemned ever more strictly by the peace-loving people of the world.

On our side, in spite of weaknesses in equipment and techniques and in the economic field, we have absolute political and moral superiority, a correct line of leadership, the strength of the people's unity, the invincible people's war, and the strong sympathy and support of the peoples throughout the world. . . .

First, we have the party's correct revolutionary line. This line is the condensed expression of the clever and creative combination of Marxist-Leninist general principles with the concrete realities of our country's revolution. This is the line of the people's national democratic revolution progressing toward socialism, befitting the case of a country that was once a colony and semifeudal state. . . . In the light of this line, the Vietnamese nation was the first among the colonies to rise up and defeat the mighty army of an imperialist power, the French imperialists, to liberate itself. The northern part of our country is also the first state to take the path of socialism in southeast Asia. . . .

Second, we are united in a bloc of all the people against the U.S. imperialists and for national salvation. The North and

South are of one mind in their determination to defeat the U.S. aggressors and their lackeys. . . . Today, our people in the South have the National Liberation Front, an organization with a broad base and a correct line and program and enjoying high prestige at home and abroad. . . .

Third, we have the invincible people's war and the experience to lead this struggle. If one can say that at present in the military field, apart from the great invention of the atomic

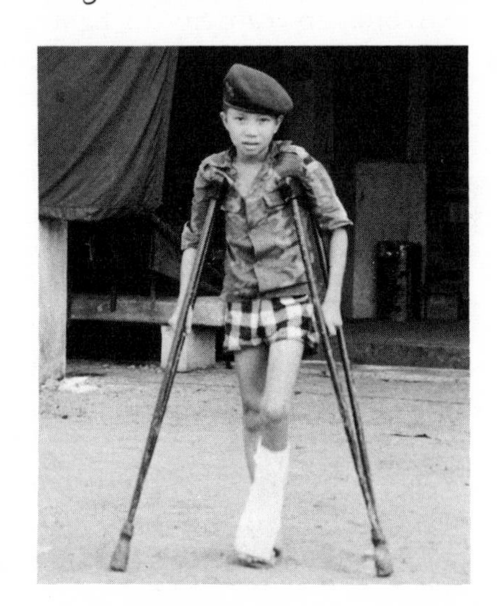

Private Ta Thai Manh convalesces from his wounds. Though barely into his teens, he wears the beret of a South Vietnamese Ranger.

(*Photo: JUSPAO-Saigon*)

weapon, there is a greater invention, the people's war, then one can safely say that the Vietnamese people have contributed to the devising and the efficient wielding of such an invincible weapon. People's war in our country has developed in the historical, political, and social conditions of Vietnam and achieved a very high standard with an extremely varied content. People's war in our country has developed according to the general law of revolutionary war but also according to the specific laws of the Vietnamese society and battlefields. Therefore, it is a nationwide and comprehensive revolutionary war, and at the same time it is a revolutionary war waged by a small nation on a small territory inhabited by a small population, having an underdeveloped economy, relying on the strength of its people's unit in the struggle, which will finally knock out an enemy originally many times stronger than itself.

People's war in Vietnam in general is a revolutionary armed struggle developing on the basis of the masses' political upsurge. Hence, the revolutionary masses' boundless strength has pervaded the revolutionary armed force and given them an extraordinary capacity to fight and win. Moreover, the outstanding characteristic of the people's war in our country at the present stage is that in the midst of the fighting, armed struggle and political struggle are very closely coordinated and are mutually helpful and interacting. Thus, the slogan "mobilize the entire people, arm the entire people, and fight the aggressors on all fronts" has become a most lively and heroic reality. . . .

Armed struggle in the South has another characteristic: In guerrilla warfare or in regular warfare, the revolutionary armed struggle is fully capable of solving the question of outdoing an enemy equipped with modern weapons, like the U.S. armed forces. In the South, not only the regular army but also the regional army and the militia and guerrillas can wipe out American and puppet troops and foil their most modern tactics. . . .

Fourth, we enjoy the warm sympathy and wholehearted support given us by the peoples of the brother socialist countries and the progressive peoples throughout the world, including the Americans.

"WHAT WE ARE FIGHTING FOR," BY *Dr. Tran Van Do*

This strongly anti-Communist view of the war, blaming it all on the North, was written by a dis-

tinguished Vietnamese. Dr. Tran Van Do served as Foreign Minister of South Vietnam on two occasions, in 1954—when he represented South Vietnam at the Geneva Conference and pleaded in vain against partition—and in 1955. This speech was delivered to the 12th SEATO *Council Meeting, April, 1967, in Washington, D.C.*

The Republic of Vietnam came into existence in the aftermath of Geneva, as a result of partition of what was known then as the State of Vietnam. Although not a signatory of the 1954 agreement on the cessation of hostilities, the Republic of Vietnam was determined to observe it loyally in the hope of contributing to the stability of the region and of saving its resources for the heavy task of reconstruction. South Vietnam did not accept the partition with a light heart. As the leader of the Vietnamese Delegation to the 1954 Geneva Conference, I made strong representations then against what I considered as a solution that "would present extremely grave disadvantages and dangers for the future."

My fears unfortunately have proved to be justified, and for thirteen years now the area has never quite recovered the stability hoped for by the signatories of the Geneva agreements.

There is little doubt that international Communism is the main actor who lurks behind the Indochinese convulsions. It supports, supplies, and directs the Viet Cong, and it trains them to use all the ghastly weapons in the service of totalitarianism, such as terrorism, sabotage, intimidation, and propaganda, and now, open armed attacks. But the revolting fact is that the North Vietnamese Government itself, a party to the Geneva agreements, has deliberately violated these agreements by initiating a war that actually makes them meaningless. Hanoi has tried in vain to conceal its omnipotent role by using the façade of a so-called "Front of Liberation." The façade progressively crumbled, showing hard-core Communist cadres and regulars from the North Vietnamese People's Army in direct action. At this point, the very admissions by Communist official media have established that the Front is nothing but an arm and an instrument of the Hanoi regime. I should like to point out that the latest documents captured from the Viet Cong stronghold in Zone C have revealed that most of the important military chiefs of the Front are simply generals of the North Vietnamese People's Army sent to the South. One of them, General Nguyen Chi Thanh, formerly Commander in Chief of the People's Militia Forces of North Vietnam, wrote in the July, 1963, issue of the *Hoc Tap* review:

> We believe that the building of a powerful North Vietnam and the revolutionary movement of the South Vietnamese people are two factors which are closely interrelated and which complement each other. The entire people of North Vietnam and of the Socialist camp stand shoulder to shoulder with the Southern people; *for them the revolution in the South is their revolution; it is the cause of world revolution.*

Since its inception, the Front has carried out faithfully all directives coming from Hanoi, including a persistent refusal to consider any attempt to promote a negotiated settlement. The activities of the Communists have increased sharply over the past few years. I wish briefly to recapitulate them now in an attempt to portray the pattern of Communist aggression in Vietnam.

Between 1962 and 1966, in order to impose their dictates, the Communists murdered over 10,000 of the civilian population, wounded 25,000 more, and abducted 35,000. Those are just accounts of individual acts of assassination and kidnapping, and do not include war casualties. By acts of terrorism, the Communists try to destroy the will of resistance among the population and impose their rule by fear.

In addition, the Communists themselves claim that they have razed from the earth about 7,500 hamlets between 1961 and 1965. Several thousand government officials, mostly civil servants in the rural areas, are assassinated and kidnapped every year. Schools, hospitals, pagodas, and churches are constantly destroyed. All those acts are aimed at preventing the Republic of Vietnam from maintaining an effective administrative apparatus and insuring development in the rural areas.

The status of the demilitarized zone [DMZ] that lies across the Seventeenth Parallel was violated by the Communists 824 times in 1962, 884 times in 1963, more than 1,000 times in 1964; and from then on, the Communists have openly used the demilitarized zone as a staging area and military passageway. The figures on the infiltration of North Vietnamese into South Vietnam show the following progression: from 4,500 in 1960 to 12,400 in 1964, 26,500 in 1965, and 73,900 in 1966. Thus, in seven years, at least 144,300 North Vietnamese have illegally infiltrated into South Vietnam.

Against this background, our request for American assistance to defend the independence of Vietnam was in full conformity with the policy of the United States as stated at Geneva. According to a declaration dated July 21, 1954, the government of the United States "would view any renewal of the aggression in violation of the Geneva agreements with grave concern and as seriously threatening international peace and security."

From another standpoint, the American assistance to Vietnam has greatly increased the confidence in the Southeast Asia Treaty Organization [SEATO] by the free nations in the area. They realized that some of its members, individually and jointly, have lived up to their obligations and assumed their responsibility with determination. The Republic of Vietnam is grateful to these members, namely Australia, New Zealand, the Philippines, Thailand, and especially the United States, who is carrying the heaviest burden among our allies.

Some critics of our common policy have expressed doubt about the possibility of defeating Communism in a situation like Vietnam. They argue that the Communists are unparalleled experts in guerrilla warfare, that the people of Vietnam seem to have resigned to accept Communist tyranny, that no amount of pacification can restore government services in the countryside, which has been firmly dominated by the Communists since the days of French colonialism.

The years since 1966 have clearly shown that the detractors and prophets of doom were wrong. First, the Vietnamese and Allied forces have won numerous battles; they have adapted themselves to the terrain, and they have found the appropriate tactics to fight this type of warfare. Enemy strongholds and staging areas have been relentlessly attacked, bombed, probed; its installations destroyed, its lifelines interrupted. A total of 55,000 Viet Cong were killed in action last year. Of course, we have to bear in mind that North Vietnam has a vast potential for manpower resources; at all times it has a reserve of about 300,000 men to send to South Vietnam. Our interdiction efforts have not been sufficient to stop the infiltration of supplies and troops altogether, but they have limited infiltration to a level with which we can deal.

"THE PEACEMAKERS," BY *Tran Van Lam* (speech, October 29, 1969)

In this speech delivered at the Vietnam Council on Foreign Affairs, Tran Van Lam, Minister of Foreign Affairs of the Republic of Vietnam, blasts the peace movement in the United States and all those who offer unsolicited advice on how to end the war in Vietnam. President Thieu did not will-

ingly send a delegation to the peace talks in Paris, and his foreign minister apparently opposes the efforts of the "peacemakers."

All things considered, the solutions put forth by peacemakers are tinted with personal considerations, and their lack of objectivity makes it difficult to accept them.

We find a little bit of all the above in the search for peace in Vietnam. This war has caused much blood and ink to flow. The diversity of opinions on this subject is unprecedented—partly because the nature of this war is deliberately made confusing by a coordinated propaganda effort throughout the world. I shall come back to this point later.

The suggestions put forth to end the war are so numerous that I can only unfold to you the most remarkable ones. I shall classify them into broad tendencies, which still persist after our side showed its good will by stopping the bombing of North Vietnam since October 31, 1968.

Let me pass very rapidly over such unpractical but touching ideas as that of a Quaker who told our consul general in San Francisco that we need only drop color photos showing the peaceful life in areas spared from the destructions of war to make the Communists abandon their weapons; or the idea of a Vietnamese mother who, worn out by the peacemakers' lack of imagination and the apparent procrastination of the governments involved in the war, urges that the people of North and South Vietnam having relatives on the other side be sent as messengers to a free area where they would shake hands, thus ending the war as if by magic.

(1) The most active peacemakers are those who are "fed up with half-measures." Against a merciless enemy who is known never to recede, they believe that the war must be brought to his land.

Our entire remaining strength could then be used to bring

Riot police march down a Saigon street to control a political demonstration. Saigon has undergone many days of political upheaval since 1964.

about peace. People like Senators John Tower and Barry Goldwater believe that only the destruction of cities, dikes, harbor installations, and military camps in the North is effective.

This idea has come up again recently, when the cessation of the bombing of North Vietnam and the redeployment of 60,000 U.S. troops have not succeeded in toning down the warlike spirit of the Communists.

(2) The more moderate peacemakers advocate a return to the 1954 Geneva agreements. The most diversified solutions can be found here. At the Paris meetings, the speeches of the chiefs of delegations show that both sides wish for a return to that agreement. However, if the Republic of Vietnam demands, in application of the agreement, an end to the hostilities, respect of the territorial integrity of neighboring countries, withdrawal of all aggressors to the other side of the

demilitarized zone, the Communists only want to retain their own version of the principles of independence, neutrality, nonalliance, and the right to self-determination. These principles are those held by a war instigator who tries to justify his aggression, and his attempts to overthrow neighboring governments in order to impose his own regime.

Neutrality and coalition are the attractive words that fascinate the peacemakers, who find in them a magic solution for all of Southeast Asia. They forget that Laos has paid a high price for it and is still denouncing the Communist violations of the 1962 Geneva agreements at the twenty-fourth meeting of the United Nations General Assembly this month.

The study of the concept that each one of us gives to these fundamental principles will bring us to understand the ideological character of the Vietnam war and the difficulties in finding a final solution. Unfortunately, peace will remain precarious as long as the world remains divided into two irreconcilable political systems.

(3) Finally, those who advocate peace without delay demand a unilateral and total withdrawal of allied troops (specifically, U.S. troops). Even if this move leaves South Vietnam in Communist hands, this is to them the only possible solution. Proclaiming that the U.S. involvement in Vietnam is a mistake, these eager beavers find in disengagement the most logical means to get out of the "quagmire."

But unconditional and immediate withdrawal or total withdrawal within a year is what the aggressors want; this explains why they are encouraging these peacemakers on this road by reducing provisionally their military activities.

A bill has been submitted to Congress by Senator Charles Goodell to limit the presidential commanding power and to impose on the chief executive a withdrawal of all troops before the end of 1970, but this bill has been rejected. We still remember the famous Mansfield plan asking for an immediate cease-fire and accelerated troop withdrawal. The ideas of the majority leader in the U.S. Senate has led to a counterattack by the State Department, which quoted a statement by President Nixon in a press conference on September 26: "The United States has made a far-reaching and comprehensive peace offer, a peace which offers mutual withdrawal of forces, internationally guaranteed cease-fires, internationally supervised elections. . . . Now it is the time for Hanoi to make the next move."

The most incredible proposal came from U.S. Senator George McGovern, who envisaged a mass exodus of three million South Vietnamese to the United States in case the quick withdrawal of allied troops leads to Communist occupation of South Vietnam.

These suggested solutions are equivalent to surrender. No U.S. President can agree to that. The pacifists have reached such extremes that some of Mr. Nixon's critics, for instance, Mr. Hubert H. Humphrey, have reversed their attitude. They now support Nixon's efforts to bring about peace. The former Secretary of Defense, Mr. Clark Clifford, and Senator Wallace Bennett have warned of the danger of a quick "liquidation" of the situation. Only the former Paris negotiators, Governor Averell Harriman and Ambassador Cyrus Vance, from whom one could expect some restraint because of their former functions, are still voicing their personal convictions in public. The main idea exposed by Mr. Vance consists of a *status quo* recognition of the territories controlled by both sides at the time of the cease-fire. This idea is not new; it has been proposed under different names such as leopard spot, territorial accommodations, and stand-still cease-fire.

The main difficulty is precisely the absolute impossibility of determining, in practice, the zones of influence in a guerrilla war where the enemy is everywhere and nowhere. The atmosphere of impatience in which the solution was formulated only makes the controversy more intense and brings confusion to an already inextricable situation.

The confusion reached its peak in the United States on Moratorium Day, October 15, 1969.

Why do so many contradictory attitudes and diversified positions for peace in Vietnam exist?

This error in judgment is the result of the ignorance of the strategy of North Vietnamese Communists, which is carried out in the battlefield as well as at the conference table.

Strange indeed is this undeclared war! For how can an aggressor declare a war since he cannot admit to his own purposes?

In spite of the capture or the rallying of a great number of Northern troops, in spite of the presence of North Vietnamese regular units in Laos, in spite of the continual flow of convoys along the so-called Ho Chi Minh trail, which is really a highway through the jungle, and in spite of bases harboring over 40,000 North Vietnamese troops in Cambodia (which has finally acknowledged this fact), North Vietnam continues to call this a war of national liberation and claims that it only gives moral support to the self-generated and self-sufficient armed rebellion of the South. North Vietnam, however, agreed to come to the conference table to negotiate peace.

The desire for peace is a genuine feeling. Taking advantage of this essentially humane sentiment, experts in psychological and political warfare have designed a scheme that could gravely disturb the normal functioning of democratic societies. In this respect, "peace movements" orchestrated by remote control constitute a strategic innovation of the same importance as guerrilla-warfare methods.

A new element interferes with the development of events that is the systematic application of "popular pressures." This means, in part, the end of the monopoly of diplomats, professionals, and technicians. For nowadays, everybody wants to be Metternich and play the role of mediator. This does not necessarily serve the cause of peace. On the contrary, the disorder that inevitably results will only make the problems confused and entangled.

In brief, this new strategy favors totalitarian regimes over democracies.

The fight against the Communists is a game of intelligence and an endurance test. As President Nguyen Van Thieu said in his message of October 6 to the National Assembly, "they know themselves that they will not become militarily stronger; but that lack of determination and impatience will weaken us, and they plan to obtain political advantages at the conference table without having to win on the battlefield. It is the defeatists on our side who encouraged the Communists to persevere in their bad faith, and who have thus prolonged the war."

One thing, however, is certain, and I conclude by quoting once more our President: "The right of self-determination of the people of South Vietnam and the integrity of our territory are not negotiable."

NATIONAL LIBERATION FRONT TEN-POINT PEACE PROPOSAL, SUBMITTED IN PARIS ON MAY 8, 1969, BY *NLF Chief Delegate Tran Buu Kiem* (in *The New York Times*, May 9, 1969)

Although "substantive" sessions of the Paris Peace Talks, including representatives of the National Liberation Front and the Saigon Government, as well as American and North Vietnamese delegates, began on January 25, 1969, very little progress has been made since then. Here is the proposal of the NLF, advocating withdrawal of all United States troops, the establishment of a coalition government in South Vietnam of all politi-

cal forces that stand for "peace, independence, and neutrality," and a step-by-step achievement of reunification through agreement between the two zones "without foreign interference." All this would obviously spell the doom of the present regime in South Vietnam.

Principles and Main Content of an Over-all Solution to the South Vietnam Problem to Help Restore Peace in Vietnam

Proceeding from a desire to reach a political solution with a view to ending the United States imperialists' war of aggression in South Vietnam and helping restore peace in Vietnam,

On the basis of the guarantee of the fundamental national rights of the Vietnamese people,

Proceeding from the fundamental principles of the 1954 Geneva agreements on Vietnam and the actual situation in Vietnam,

On the basis of the political program and the five-point position of the South Vietnam National Liberation Front, which keeps with the four-point stand of the government of the Democratic Republic of North Vietnam,

The South Vietnam National Liberation Front sets forth the principles and main content of an over-all solution to the South Vietnam problem to help restore peace in Vietnam as follows:

(1)

To respect the Vietnamese people's fundamental national rights, that is, independence, sovereignty, unity and territorial integrity, as recognized by the 1954 Geneva agreements on Vietnam.

(2)

The United States Government must withdraw from South Vietnam all United States troops, military personnel, arms and war matériel of the other foreign countries of the United States camp without posing any condition whatsoever; liquidate all United States military bases in South Vietnam; renounce all encroachments on the sovereignty, territory and security of South Vietnam and the Democratic Republic of Vietnam.

(3)

The Vietnamese people's right to fight for the defense of their fatherland is the sacred, inalienable right to self-defense of all peoples. The question of the Vietnamese armed forces in South Vietnam shall be resolved by the Vietnamese parties among themselves.

(4)

The people of South Vietnam shall settle themselves their own affairs without foreign interference. They shall decide themselves the political regime of South Vietnam through free and democratic general elections; a constituent assembly will be set up, a constitution worked out and a coalition government of South Vietnam installed, reflecting national concord and the broad union of all social strata.

(5)

During the period intervening between the restoration of peace and the holding of general elections, neither party shall impose its political regime on the people of South Vietnam.

The political forces representing the various social strata and political tendencies in South Vietnam that stand for peace, independence, and neutrality—including those persons who, for political reasons, have to live abroad—will enter into talks to set up a provisional coalition government based on the principle of equality, democracy, and mutual respect with a view to achieving a peaceful, independent, democratic, and neutral South Vietnam.

The provisional coalition government is to have the following tasks:

A. To implement the agreement to be concluded on the withdrawal of the troops of the United States and the other foreign countries of the American camp.

B. To achieve national concord, and a broad union of all social strata, political forces, nationalities, religious communities, and all persons, no matter what their political beliefs and their past may be, provided they stand for peace, independence, and neutrality.

C. To achieve broad democratic freedoms—freedom of speech, freedom of the press, freedom of assembly, freedom of belief, freedom to form political parties and organizations, freedom to demonstrate, and so on; to set free those persons jailed on political grounds; to prohibit all acts of terror, reprisal, and discrimination against people having collaborated with either side, and who are now in the country or abroad, as provided for by the 1954 Geneva agreements on Vietnam.

D. To heal the war wounds, restore and develop the economy, to restore the normal life of the people, and to improve the living conditions of the laboring people.

E. To hold free and democratic general elections in the whole of South Vietnam with a view to achieving the South Vietnam people's right to self-determination, in accordance with the content of point 4 mentioned above.

(6)

South Vietnam will carry out a foreign policy of peace and neutrality:

To carry out a policy of good neighborly relations with the Kingdom of Cambodia on the basis of respect for her independence, sovereignty, neutrality, and territorial integrity within her present borders; to carry out a policy of good neighborly relations with the Kingdom of Laos on the basis of respect for the 1962 Geneva agreements on Laos.

To establish diplomatic, economic, and cultural relations with all countries, irrespective of political and social regime, including the United States, in accordance with the five principles of peaceful coexistence: mutual respect for independence, sovereignty, and territorial integrity, nonaggression, noninterference in internal affairs, equality, and mutual benefit, peaceful coexistence, to accept economic and technical aid with no political conditions attached from any country.

(7)

The reunification of Vietnam will be achieved step by step, by peaceful means, through discussions and agreement between the two zones, without foreign interference.

Pending the peaceful reunification of Vietnam, the two zones shall re-establish normal relations in all fields on the basis of mutual respect.

The military demarcation line between the two zones at the Seventeenth Parallel, as provided for by the 1954 Geneva agreements, is only of a provisional character and does not constitute in any way a political or territorial boundary. The two zones shall reach agreement on the status of the demilitarized zone, and work out modalities for movements across the provisional military demarcation line.

(8)

As provided for in the 1954 Geneva agreements on Vietnam, the two zones, North and South Vietnam, shall undertake to refrain from joining any military alliance with foreign countries, not allow any foreign country to maintain military bases, troops, and military personnel on their respective soil, and not recognize the protection of any country or military alliance or bloc.

(9)

To resolve the aftermath of the war:

A. The parties will negotiate the release of soldiers captured in the war.

B. The United States government must bear full responsibility for the losses and devastations it has caused to the Vietnamese people in both zones.

(10)

The parties shall reach agreement on an international supervision about the withdrawal from South Vietnam of the troops, military personnel, arms, and war matériel of the United States and the other foreign countries of the American camp.

The principles and content of the over-all solution expounded above form an integrated whole. On the basis of these principles and content, the parties shall reach understanding to the effect of concluding agreements on the abovementioned questions with a view to ending the war in South Vietnam and contributing to restoring peace in Vietnam.

Tra Dan Xuan, the traditional spring tea ceremony, is offered at the Tet to the memory of an ancestor. The flowering narcissuses symbolize the promise of a new year. *(Photo: Pham Van Mui)*

PART THREE

A Poetic People: Literature and Art

INTRODUCTION TO VIETNAMESE CULTURE

François Sully

The Vietnamese people take pride in their age-old culture, in their traditional love for education and study, which is in no way less ardent than their desire for national cultural identity. The main trait of Vietnamese culture is its astonishing faculty to assimilate foreign contributions, very much like the way our modern Western culture has assimilated the heritage of former Greek, Latin, and Nordic civilizations. This process of continuous assimilation and transformation is what makes a culture dynamic and modern. When Vietnamese need to coin a new word that does not yet exist in their own vocabulary, they borrow a root word from either Chinese or French and transform it, adapt it, until it looks and sounds totally Vietnamese. The Vietnamese word for *cement,* which they write *xi mang,* comes—of course—from the French *ciment*. So is the word *o to but,* which comes from *autobus*. Chinese language has provided words such as *chinh phu* (government) and *ngoai truong* (foreign affairs ministry).

The same Chinese influence, says Professor Truong Buu Lam, extends to Vietnamese literature, but this influence has been adapted for Vietnamese use. Let us take a concrete example: the writing system. Vietnamese for centuries studied Chinese characters. They wrote their books in Chinese characters, and they read Chinese books, but very few spoke

Two oboists play accompaniment for the Imperial Ballet of Hue. Traditional music, based on the Chinese five-tone scale, survives in Central Vietnam but is disappearing in the modern cities.

Chinese, for the simple reason that they spoke Vietnamese instead. They were in need of a system of writing that would enable them to write Vietnamese, so they invented the *nom* characters, which were a combination of Chinese characters adapted to writing Vietnamese words. Most of the *nom* characters consisted of two Chinese characters. One gave the meaning and the other gave the pronunciation of the word.

The same phenomenon occurred later when, in the seventeenth century, European missionaries Romanized the Vietnamese spoken language. Then, instead of writing with Chinese characters, as with the *nom* characters, they used the Roman alphabet, and wrote Vietnamese phonetically, with accent marks to indicate tones.

Therefore, Vietnamese authors were right to a certain extent when they said "our people long ago established Vietnam as an independent nation with its own civilization. We have our own mountains and rivers, our own customs and traditions, and these are different from those of the foreign country to the north, China."

The Vietnamese are primarily a literary people: Their tonal language combines subtle weaving with musical sound, and they use it exquisitely. In ancient times, their poetry and prose was chanted and declaimed, in order to derive full dramatic and aural effect from the rising and falling of the tones. Their legends and traditional poems reveal the romanticism and sensitivity of the Vietnamese soul.

LITERATURE OF THE PAST

"THE COMPLAINT OF A BEAUTIFUL GIRL IN A KING'S HAREM," BY *Nguyen Gia Thieu* (1741–98)

This famous poem of 356 verses expresses the griefs of a beautiful girl who in her youth became the king's favorite. For a short while, she enjoyed happiness, fame, and love. Later deserted, she lived in a harem with 3,000 other royal concubines.

In ancient Vietnam, it was the custom for kings to maintain harems with hundreds of young concubines who had been selected for their charm and outstanding beauty. It was then an honor and a source of pride for a family to have one of their daughters among the king's concubines, for she was often able to obtain royal favors and privileges for her relatives. The last Vietnamese king to maintain a harem was Khai Dinh, who reigned from 1916 to 1925. Concubines were presented to the king by mandarins of the court who thought to please him. Some of the girls remained all their lives confined to a harem without ever being visited by their royal husband.

It was then that the odalisques *gave utterance to their complaints and sorrows. Sometimes, their grief-imbued words would be used in a beautiful poem conveying the poignant fate of a sensitive and unfortunate girl, whose happiness was as ephemeral as the life of a butterfly in summer.*

I was a beautiful talented girl.
I furtively think of the early days of my life:
Full-grown, I was like a rose in the daylight.
The rose hadn't opened its corolla to smile,
Other flowers soon faded and became vile.

Things have changed.
Now, things have changed: He has abandoned me;
Once a wise lady, I now become a little silly.
Oh my august friend, you have so flighty a heart,
Now, I regret my spring and endure this ill luck.

I think of the moment when, in the Tan palace,
You picked a willow branch, in its early freshness.
The vernal gown I wore when I was close to you
Is still here, to testify to our tender love.

Now, my lord, you have resolutely disdained me,
So, unexpectedly, friendless I've turned out to be.
Oh Heaven, why do you challenge me by confining
Me in this hell, with a lamp growing dim?

I care about my growing age, like a faint moon,
Or a fallen flower, which can attract no one.
How sad my love is and how charmless the world.

My pretty face worried the hearts of other belles,
My lovely glance could even collapse a citadel.
When my graceful shadow loomed up through a blind,
Plants and weeds would have their sexual instincts aroused.

Seduced, a fish would dive deep into the waters,
A high-flying swallow would feel dizzy and falter.
By my heavenly charms, a flower would be enticed,
Miss Tay-Thi would be dazed, Miss Moon would be surprised.

I was famous, in wait for an idyll.
My gifts and beauty were famous in the kingdom,
The suitors increasingly loitered near my home.
They had only heard of my charms and not seen me,
Yet, their passion had risen fiercely.

I was passionately loved, but my happiness was ephemeral.
Frequently, in moonlight, he gently embraced me,
And often, in the palace, we laughed together lovingly.
He was very pleased with my natural grace,
I was equally pretty without rouging my face.

The monarch cherished me like a precious sapphire,
He coddled me and yielded to all my desires.
Indeed, a woman's beauty, having no venom,
Can poison everyone and overthrow a kingdom!

"KIM VAN KIEU," BY *Nguyen Du*

The Kim Van Kieu *is Vietnam's best-known and best-loved epic poem. It was written by Nguyen Du, a Vietnamese scholar-mandarin-diplomat born in 1765 to a family of mandarins. The poem has crossed political and generation barriers and remains today the most often quoted literary work in Vietnam.*

The plot is based on an ancient Chinese story. The title combines the names of the three central characters: Thuy Kieu, the heroine, Kim Trong, her beloved, and Thuy Van, her sister. Thuy Kieu, a gentle beauty living in the sixteenth century, renounced her love for Kim Trong, and sold herself into prostitution in order to save her family's finances and honor. Her life became a succession of misfortunes and betrayals.

Fifteen years after the family tragedy forced her to become a courtesan, the once beautiful Kieu found refuge in a Buddhist temple. There, she was discovered by Kim, her boyhood suitor, who had been roaming the country looking for her. Despite Kim's marriage to Kieu's younger sister Thuy Van, his feeling toward his first love remained unchanged and he dutifully asked Kieu to become his second wife. But Kieu knew herself to be but "a stained flower" and pleaded with Kim not to "try to recover the perfume that has been dropped on the ground." Reluctantly, they both agreed that marriage would be unwise, and they vowed to remain friends for life.

The night
wore on; the moon at its Zenith, but still
not half of what they wished to say
had been said of all their suffering,
all their joy; loose cords
that held back bed curtains fell
and in the gentle lamplight, her
curves seemed rounder, her color
fresher, so did old lovers meet again,
the flower that once had blossomed

and the bee that had lit upon it
happy once more together!

Kieu becoming serious again, said,
"As for my own self, it is of no consequence
this useless body is of small use
to you; I am grateful that you
have remembered our past love and
show me your favor still; now
in a small way I have complied
with your desire, yet at heart
am I already ashamed; after all
I have done, surely I am no longer
good to look at! In future
best should we, for the sake
of honor keep our love on the level
of simple good friendship,
for should you try to recover the
perfume that has dropped
on the ground, or search
for a flower when the season
is over, so will you draw notice
to my shame, and then maybe
hatred will supplant the love
that burns between us; your love
for me has always been great, yet
I was not good to you; in our love
our very faithfulness has wrought us
harm! Now, should you be anxious
for your posterity, my sister
is with you; there is no need
to rely on me; hereafter the best way
I can be true to you,
is in thoughtful friendship:
you should help me in this rather

than crush my resolve underfoot:
we are bound by much, but for you
there can be but little interest
in a fading flower;"
Kim replied,
"We pledged ourselves to each other,
suddenly we were separated, as
fish from water, as birds
from the sky; your absence has given me
deep suffering; I am sure that after
all the promises exchanged, you too
have suffered equally; through life
and death we swore to maintain
our love; now as we meet again
we must make each other happy,

Classical Vietnamese theater is deeply influenced by the traditions of Chinese opera. Costuming is elaborate and symbolic. The stage sets are extremely simple and employ scenic conventions to indicate time and place.

bringing fullness to our love:
you, still graceful, supple, like
a willow, young and green; how now
can we two not taste of all
that our union brings? For me
I know that the mirror of your soul
is pure and unstained by the dust
of the world: all through the years
has my love for you but deepened
ever searching for you, even though
it has been like the hopeless groping
for a needle at the bottom of the sea!
It is because of this great love
engraved as it is so deeply in all
we treasure, rather than to any thought
of lightness, that I ever dared
to go on hoping somehow we two
would come together once more! surely
in the face of all of this, it is
unnecessary we share the same bed
to be counted husband and wife!"

With these words, did Kieu
putting her gown straight, arranging
her hair, bow low before him,
expressing her gratitude, saying
"Should now in my remaining days
that side of our love be removed
it will be due to your nobility
so high above that of ordinary folk;
what you have said comes from your
inmost being! our understanding
is sincere and full; now you have
thought much for my welfare, protecting me
restoring my life its dignity!"

Reading Notes, by Nguyen Khac Vien

For the foreign reader who has to enjoy Kieu *through a translation, we should like to make one remark. It is possible in a translation to find adequate rhythms, but the translator still finds before him an insurmountable obstacle when he tries to translate from the Vietnamese into a "toneless" language, French or English, for example.*

Vietnamese lends itself admirably to multiple harmonic combinations; each syllable can be pronounced on six different tones to mean six different things. It is enough to combine these tones and modulate certain words to turn a sentence into a verse and plain speech into a song. How to render in a toneless language this music of tones that evokes so many feelings in the hearts of Vietnamese readers?

The obstacle is truly insuperable when those phonetic combinations aim not only at a musical effect of rhythm but also a descriptive effect. There exists in Vietnamese a category of words made up of repeated syllables often when the syllable is repeated, a change is made either concerning the tone, the consonant, the vowel, or the diphthong, and this slight modification is enough to give to the meaning of the word an indefinable shade.

A wind that is hiu hiu *is a light breeze which hardly ripples the surface of a pond, but when it turns* hiu hat, *one knows that its breath already carries a touch of cold. When sails loom* thap thoang, *it means that they appear at one time and disappear at another and that, receiving the sunlight under varying angles, they look now brilliant, now lusterless. When a lover feels* bang khuang, *he is at the same time much more and much less than "out of sorts"; when he is obsessed with the memory of his sweetheart and when every beat of his own heart evokes reminiscences of her, the poet uses the word* canh canh, *and the translator has to resign himself to some clumsy paraphrase. Almost the whole of this music—now light and subtle like a spring breeze, now breaking loose in a cascade of notes, in turn muffled and sonorous, at times gay and triumphant, and at others sad and poignant—disappears from even the best translations.*

"WHY EVERY AMERICAN SHOULD READ KIM VAN KIEU," BY *Tran Van Dinh*, adapted from an article in *The Washingtonian*, September, 1968

Author Tran Van Dinh believes that Kim Van Kieu *reflects the mentality, soul, and aspiration of the Vietnamese people and, as such, reveals more of the motivation of Vietnamese guerrillas than any document captured on the battlefield. If only for this reason, Dinh suggests that all U.S. civilian and military officials should read, study, and analyze* Kim Van Kieu *instead of basing their judgment on statistics.*

Author Tran Van Dinh, after serving in high posts with the "liberation army" in Vietnam and Laos, came South following partition and joined the South Vietnamese foreign service. He was chargé d'affaires in Washington in 1963 but subsequently left government service and now resides in Washington, D.C.

Thuy Kieu, the heroine and central figure of *Kim Van Kieu*, is Vietnam: beautiful, talented, condemned by her pale fate. Kim Trong, her chivalrous lover, is the Vietnamese dream of *thong nhut*, of the unity of the Vietnamese nation that somehow the Vietnamese have never attained. Even if it is attained, it would only be by compromise, an imperfect unity: Thuy Kieu did not marry Kim Trong, although they did finally meet again. Her sister, Thuy Van, "a moon-faced beauty," is rather dull and unromantic, a suburban housewife, so to speak. And she was the compromise.

But, above all, *Kim Van Kieu* is the embodiment of the Vietnamese soul, the Vietnamese psyche. A friend of mine, a poet and writer who visited the United States, said to me when we discussed U.S. policy in Vietnam: "Had President Johnson, Mr. Rusk, Mr. Rostow, Mr. McNamara, the U.S. ambassador in Saigon, and all of the U.S. civilian and military personnel in Vietnam read *Kim Van Kieu*, instead of basing their judgments on meaningless facts and statistics, they would have avoided many serious and even fatal mistakes. The situation in our country would be different."

"But how can they read and understand it?" I asked.

"Well, that is the difficulty," my friend replied. "And that is why we as a nation survive until today. Nobody really could understand *Kim Van Kieu* but the Vietnamese. Perhaps a Jew can understand Vietnamese history; an Irishman, the Vietnamese romantic mind; the Russian, the Vietnamese pessimism; and the Italian, the Vietnamese sense of optimism and drama. No one, no American, can be a mixture of all these," he sighed.

President Ho Chi Minh and Premier Pham Van Dong of North Vietnam have often told foreign visitors that "we Vietnamese revolutionaries are romantic and optimistic." They just told them half of the truth.

The Vietnamese national behavior is basically and deeply formed by Buddhism, structured by the ethics of Confucianism, and mystified by Taoism. These were the three currents of religion and philosophy that penetrated Vietnam two thousand years ago, molded the Vietnamese character, and, in turn, were modified and influenced by the political and military fortunes of the country. Buddhism is erroneously pictured in the West as a religion of renunciation, of passivism, even of fatalism. In fact, Buddhism recognizes the realities of human sufferings, confronts them, and tries to solve them. It accepts the intimate relations of cause and effect of the laws of Karma.

Each man is born with a Karma, which in Vietnamese is *so* or *menh,* meaning fate or destiny, which is the sum of not only his past but also his present actions. In other words, man is what he was and what he is. But, at the same time, man is not the eternal prisoner of his Karma: He can change it by correct and right behavior and good deeds. A Buddhist, therefore, relies on himself primarily for his own salvation, and, knowing the causes of man's sufferings, he is tolerant and attentive to the shortcomings of his fellow man.

The Vietnamese believe that a man's *tuong* (physiognomy) is not as important as his *so,* and his *so* is not as important as his *duc* (good deeds). Buddhism is a creatively active religion that opens hopeful alternatives, and that favors man's struggle (*dau tranh*) for his betterment. The Viet Cong often use the words *dau tranh* in their pamphlets and programs.

Confucianism is not a religion, as it is principally concerned with social ethics. Confucianism reaches for order, not for salvation. Taoism admits a "universal order" and the participation of men in this universal order. Because of this concept of a higher order of the universe, Taoism was largely misunderstood and degenerated into all kinds of superstitious practices—ways to implore *troi* (heaven) to solve man's problems. The usual Vietnamese exclamation is *Troi, Phat* (Heaven, Buddha).

Implacable Destiny

Thuy Kieu faced the brutalities of her Karma, the realities of life, and struggled with them to make them better. She sold herself to save her family, acting in true Buddhist compassion for the community of man and in the true Confucian ethic of filial piety. In the darkest and most desperate moments of her life, she managed to keep her confidence in her good deeds, which she thought would eventually change her Karma, her *bac menh* (pale fate).

When they describe the courage of the Viet Cong and the North Vietnamese on the battlefields or in suicide raids, most Western journalists call them fanatics. But they are not. They face the realities of the Karma of their country, which is the sum of the Karmas of all individuals, and they are determined to change it. The Vietnamese national Karma is marked by division among Vietnamese, by foreign invasions and interventions. That Karma is indeed hard, the Vietnamese national fate is indeed pale, the Vietnamese national destiny is indeed implacable.

Some thoughtful Vietnamese relate this Karma to the past conquests by Vietnam, often carried on with much bloodshed and brutality. From the eleventh century until the early nineteenth century, Vietnam, in her forceful *nam tien* (march to the south) destroyed and exterminated peoples and civilizations. The Kingdom of Champa, a flourishing state, disappeared from the map at the end of the fifteenth century. The Vietnamese military expeditions into Laos and Cambodia were usually bloody and ruthless. But today, the Viet Cong and the North Vietnamese are not giving up: They are convinced that fighting against foreign armies will change the Karma of their country for the better. The South Vietnamese soldier, although Vietnamese, is not fighting as well; he is outside the stream of Vietnamese history, he is associated with the foreigners who divided Vietnam. He is feeling, in a way, less Vietnamese.

When the United States bombs North Vietnam, the North Vietnamese believe that the United States is accumulating wrong deeds that eventually will turn against it. By resisting American pressures, they believe they serve a just cause. The Viet Cong and the North Vietnamese soldiers accept death in order to allow the Vietnamese rivers and mountains to remain green, the Vietnamese earth and water to endure. When Thuy Kieu sold herself to save her family, she said: "It is better that I should sacrifice myself alone, It matters little if a flower falls if the tree could keep its leaves green."

The principal themes of *Kim Van Kieu* are life and fate, the inherent contradiction between *tai* (talent or know-how) and *tai* (disaster, misfortune), the cause and effect relationship between *tai* and *menh* (fate, Karma). The novel opens with these sentences: "Within the span of a hundred years of human existence, What a bitter struggle is waged between talent and fate," and concludes with: "When one is endowed with talent, do not rely on it."

Austerity Is Attractive

To the Vietnamese, the United States indeed has *tai* (the know-how), but it is courting with *tai* (disaster). So they are reluctant to be near disaster, to be impressed by it, or to be associated with it. In Vietnam, the United States displays plenty of *tai*—air bases, buildings, and machinery—but the Buddhist concept, the Confucian ethic, and the Taoist concept of universal harmony and universal order totally disregard material wealth. In the Vietnamese hierarchy of values, a rich man is a *troc phu* (filthy rich), and a poor scholar is *thanh ban* (immaculate poor). The traditional Vietnamese social order followed this scale: first, the *si* (scholars, men of letters); second, the *nong* (peasants, farmers); third, the *cong* (workers); fourth, the *thuong* (businessmen, merchants); and fifth, and last, the *binh* (soldiers). It is too bad that the huge American military commitment has increasingly alienated the intellectuals, destroyed the life of the peasantry, and based itself on the merchants and soldiers. Thuy Kieu herself was a victim of money, of corrupted officials who asked for bribes: "To bribe the officials here and to circumvent the authorities there, Three hundred gold taels are necessary to arrive at a satisfactory settlement."

When the United States pours money into Vietnam, creating in the process hordes of corrupted officials and generals, when the big Americans walk among the frail and slender Vietnamese in the cities and in the countryside, they create a feeling of resentment and suspicion. There are, no doubt, among the thousands of Vietnamese bar girls in Saigon, those who think of themselves as modern, mini–Thuy Kieus, longing for Kim Trong, who may be the distant image of President Ho Chi Minh in the North or, more likely, the Viet Cong agitation cadre in the town. Some bar girls contribute generously to the "Viet Cong" funds for that reason. Those who marry the rich GI for money have to put on airs. They are called *me my* (mother of the American). Even the word *my* (which means "beautiful") has been distorted to *meo* (deformed, ugly).

When, in the summer of 1966, the Saigon regime used American tanks and planes to suppress the Buddhists in the austere and intellectual city of Hue (as represented by the militant monk Thich Tri Quang, who refuses to ride in a motor car), a great number of Vietnamese concluded that the materialistic Americans are in Vietnam to destroy the ascetic good men of the country. The same feeling was aroused with the arrest and imprisonment of teachers and students, the "immaculate poor" of the Vietnamese society.

The disdain for soldiers, as well as for physically big persons, can be seen in the description of Tu Hai, the rebel, in *Kim Van Kieu*. He was "an imposing man with a tiger mustache [Vietnamese, especially old people, grow beards, not mustaches], a swallow jaw [very strong], a pair of eyebrows like silkworms; he was five decimeters broad-shouldered and ten meters high." Although the old Chinese and Vietnamese meter is about one-third of the modern one, it is obvious that Nguyen Du purposely exaggerated Tu Hai's physical stature. Thuy Kieu did not love him; she used him. To her he was a *vu phu* (a man who uses force, a rude man) and he was not the scholar Kim Trong was.

Reunification: Difficult Dream

Vietnam has had a good crop of military heroes, but they have all been intellectuals and scholars. Marshal Tran Hung Dao, who defeated the Mongolians three times in the thirteenth century, wrote books; Marshal Nguyen Van Thanh, who helped Emperor Gia Long to unify Vietnam in 1802, has left the most beautiful "funeral oration to the dead soldiers" in Vietnamese epic literature; General Vo Nguyen Giap, commander in chief of the North Vietnamese army and the architect of victory at Dien Bien Phu, was a professor of history.

When the United States talks about an independent South Vietnam it deeply hurts the Vietnamese dream of *Thong Nhat*, of unity, the Kim Trong dream. No one in Vietnam could advocate the permanent division of the country. Article I of the 1967 constitution of South Vietnam says: "Vietnam is an independent country and territorially indivisible." Article CVII of the same constitution stipulates that "This article and Article I cannot be nullified or amended." But, as in *Kim Van Kieu*, the dream of unity will have to be satisfied with a compromise.

"VIETNAMESE EPIC LITERATURE," BY *Kim Chi* (in *Asia*, December, 1953)

Such is the mystical feeling of the Vietnamese for the epic poem Kim Van Kieu *that they sometimes inadvertently give the foreigner the impression that only this poem is worthy of intense admiration. Here, author Kim Chi attempts to dispel this misconception by quoting from another type of literature, that devoted to heroic battle subjects.*

Speaking of Vietnamese literature, one immediately thinks of Nguyen Du's marvelous poem, beautiful enough to stand comparison with any masterpiece in world literature. *Kim Van Kieu* is an inestimable treasure that belongs to our entire people; it is the song of the Vietnamese soul, the song of a race that understands how noble are the family and domestic virtues and that has a delicate and subtle love of nature. This is a wonderful poem, in which every line is a jewel for scholars, although its beauty is accessible to all. *Kim Van Kieu* arouses secret echoes among the roughest of us and at every stage of our lives.

Yet it would be unjust to reserve all our admiration for this perfect masterpiece, and the beauty of *Kim Van Kieu* should not make us forget that our people also possess an epic literature that counts among the treasures of our patrimony.

Nguyen Du's work touches our sensibilities and intelligence, but our epic poems reveal the heroic soul of Vietnam and her love of liberty and independence. It is in these works that we find evidence of our glorious past. Vietnam is saturated with Confucian wisdom and Buddhist humility and does not always grant the same importance to material things and perishable buildings as do other nations. It is not in inert metals or proud stones that she recalls her greatness, but rather through the magic of words. The sublime examples that have made the pride of our nation are handed down from generation to generation by means of the word.

Among all the messages that we have received from our ancestors through the centuries, a special place must be given to the proclamation of General Tran Quoc Tuan to his lieutenants and his men before his decisive victory over the Mongols. This masterpiece of eloquence is nearly eight centuries old and remains one of the summits of our literature. Patriotism, fidelity to the prince, contempt for childish pleasures, and disdain of shameful compromises are expressed with soldierly roughness and such ardor and conviction that the reader is transported and moved to the bottom of his heart. Here is a typical passage:

> Thus, your master is dishonored and you care nothing for it! You enjoy cock-fighting; gambling is your favorite pleasure; you enjoy the pleasures of the countryside, you allow yourselves to be softened by the love of your wives and children. Will the claws of your cocks pierce the leather shields of the enemy when he attacks? Will all your cunning at gambling defeat his strategy? When this happens, not only will the king's lands be invaded, but you will lose your own wealth. We shall not only be humiliated in the present, but our shame will be perpetuated through centuries to come. . . . How could you find any happiness then?

We can measure the strength and vigor of this language when we remember that, at the moment when Tran Quoc Tuan was thus addressing his troops, the hordes of the Kublai were sweeping victoriously from the Mongolian steppes over all Europe and all Asia, and that our people were alone, in the whole continent, to oppose this monstrous onslaught. As Attila was stopped in the Catalaunic fields, the Mongols were stopped at Kiep Bac by a people resolute to defend its independence and survive. One man personified this resolution: Tran Quoc Tuan. It is thus that his message to us finds an irresisitible response in our hearts.

Another masterpiece of our epic literature is the famous funeral oration pronounced by Marshal Nguyen Van Thanh, companion-in-arms of Emperor Gia Long, in memory of the officers and men who died to found the empire. Certain passages of this magnificent composition, like the following description of a battle, form unforgettable frescoes:

> Some of them, surging from amidst the ardent rush of horsemen, dashed forward to tear the flag from the enemy. Alas! Though their courage was of gold, their luck was of base metal. Their lives were swept away, like the light fluff from the *hong* bird, by a stray bullet, a wandering arrow. Others, standing at the poop of their ships, would have disarmed the adversary. They were true to their honor as soldiers at the price of their lives, and the waves carried away the bodies of these heroes.

Let us also quote this passage, in which we feel the emotion of a chief who loved his men, when he remembers his fallen comrades: "Your hundred battles were a single glorious arena, in which neither life nor death existed in face of your courage and heroism. Thousands of years passed before this unique occasion came about, before we met under the same flag. How is it that, although we were together when the encounter began, you did not see its end?"

We could quote yet other poems to the glory of the warrior, who is spared the miseries of old age. We will stop here, however, believing that, if literature is the faithful expression of the hopes and virtues of a nation, it may be said that the Vietnamese people yield to none in gallantry and courage.

COMPLAINT OF A WARRIOR'S WIFE, BY *Doan Thi Diem*

Doan Thi Diem (1705–48) came from a family of scholars in North Vietnam's Bac Ninh Province, near Hanoi. Early in her youth, she demonstrated a surprising talent for poetry. Vietnam was then torn by devastating feudal wars. When a contemporary poet produced a long poem in Chinese characters on the war, Doan Thi Diem was so moved that she wrote a new version in the Vietnamese language. It was named Complaint of a Warrior's Wife. *Her translation, immediately regarded as of far superior quality than the original poem, became a classic of Vietnamese poetry, praised for the perfection and nobility of its verses. Streets in Saigon and Hanoi have been named after Doan Thi Diem, Vietnam's national lady poet. Even today,* Complaint of a Warrior's Wife *carries a familiar ring to many Vietnamese women separated from their husbands by the war.*

The wind screams and howls over our ancestors' remains.
The moon darts her last pale rays
On the frozen masks of the fighters.
How many were you, fighters, glorious dead?
Who is painting your face, evoking your memory?

On the soil of our country
War has caused so much destruction
That at their sight, the traveler feels pity!

To age on the battlefield is the fate of heroes;
General Ban Sieu * went home with white hair.

I pity you for suffering a thousand sores, a thousand dead.
With a sword, a harness as your only weapons
You defy the wind-swept plains
You climb over mountains under the moonlight
A thousand times you throw your arrow, riding your horse
A thousand times you storm the enemy's ramparts!

How difficult to climb is the path to glory
One tires himself vainly without taking rest.
Alas, here I am, locked in my bedroom, alone
And you, far beyond the horizon.
To whom may I confide the sorrows of my heart

O Lord! to live in seclusion is my destiny as a woman
But to live on the road, should it be yours?
I hoped to spend my life with you
As a fish lives with the water.
How could I imagine
That you will be the cloud carried by the wind
While I will linger like the still water.

* General Ban Sieu is a Chinese warrior who fought for thirty years in foreign countries, only to return to China, after vanquishing fifty vassal states, as a white-haired old man.

WRITINGS OF WAR AND PEACE

A BUDDHIST PRAYER FOR PEACE, BY *Thich Nhat Hanh* (delivered in Paris, 1969)

Written by monk Thich Nhat Hanh, whose letter to the late Rev. Martin Luther King appears in an earlier section, A Buddhist Prayer for Peace *contains the essence of the Vietnamese Buddhist attitude toward the present events in Vietnam. Primarily contemplative in their form of worship, the monks pray so that Vietnam can free herself from the disruptive seductions imported from abroad since, in their view, these political seductions are responsible for the fratricidal war. The monks pray the Lord Buddha to inspire their own thoughts with words that can recreate harmony among Vietnamese, so that all Vietnamese, from North and South alike, can once again learn to live in peace under one roof.*

In beauty, on the Lotus is seated
Lord Buddha, in his quiet strength.
This disciple, pure-hearted, calm
With his hands forming a lotus,
Respectfully faces the Master
To offer his sincerest prayer.

Thich Nhat Hanh (*Photo: Associated Press*)

I pay respect to the Buddhas
From ten different directions, following the rites,
For our suffering, please show compassion.
Our land at war for twenty years
Vietnam, divided land
Vietnam, land of tears.

Blood and bones of young and old
Mothers weep till their tears are dry
While their sons on faraway fields
Leave their vitals decaying
A country's beauty torn apart
Tears and blood flowing everywhere
Brothers killing each other
For alien seducers.

I pay respect to the Buddhas

From each of the ten directions
For love of our people, have compassion
Guide Vietnam unto herself
To see only one house–North and South
Harboring compassion, brotherhood
Transforming separate interests
To love's acceptance of us all
I pray that the Master's compassion
Will help us forget the hate we bear in ourselves
I pray Buddhisatva Avalokitesvara
That from the soil of Vietnam
Flowers may bloom again.

Therefore, in pious veneration
I offer the essence of my heart
For the transformation of the Karma
That all may see the spirit flower
That wisdom lighten every heart
I pay respect to the great Sakya
Immense in vows and in compassion
I vow my solemn determination
To keep in mind only those thoughts
Which will enhance our love and trust
To let my hands perform only those deeds
Which will build one community.
And from my lips allow only those words
Bringing harmony and concord

I pray to transfer all my merits to my country
So peace can come to Vietnam
And so help every one of us
Achieve the fervent wish of his heart.

"O! YOUTH," National Anthem of the Republic of Vietnam, BY *Luu Huu Phuoc*

For the youth of Vietnam, 1943 was a period of great nationalist fervor. Luu Huu Phuoc, a student at the French-run University of Hanoi wrote for his friends a stirring song that he called Thanh Nien Oi (O! Youth). *The song became so popular among Vietnamese students that they adopted it as their official hymn. Later, when Vietnam became an independent country, Emperor Bao Dai made* O! Youth *the national anthem of Vietnam. Then, in 1954, Bao Dai went into exile in France. Luu Huu Phuoc became a talented composer of music in Hanoi. In July, 1969, Phuoc was appointed Minister for Culture and Information in South Vietnam's Provisional Revolutionary Government, the political arm of the Viet Cong movement. Ironically, his song has remained the national anthem of the rival Saigon-based Republic of Vietnam. Luu Huu Phuoc was born in Can Tho, an important city in the Mekong Delta.*

Youth! arise to the Motherland's call
Of a same heart, let us lead the way
Let us remember the centuries of our history.
From the North to the South, let us unite like brothers
Of one heart, young and pure like crystal
We shall not spare our ardent blood, let us try again
No risk, no obstacle will stop us
Despite a thousand dangers, unshakable remains our courage,

On the new path, our eyes span the horizon
Our young souls, who can bind them?
Youth! Till the end, this is our resolve,
Youth! To give ourselves totally is our oath
Forward, together, for the glory of the motherland
Let us never forget that we are heirs to the Lac Long.*

NATIONAL ANTHEM OF THE DEMOCRATIC REPUBLIC OF VIETNAM: "TIEN QUANG CA" (in *Breaking Our Chains: Documents of the Vietnamese Revolution of August, 1945* [Hanoi, 1960])

Tien Quang Ca (Marching to the Front) *was composed during the struggle against the Japanese and French. It was adopted as the national anthem by the Provisional Government of the Democratic Republic of Vietnam (DRV) in the first days of its formation, and by the National Assembly of the DRV in its second session in November, 1946.*

Verse 1

Soldiers of Vietnam, we go forward!
With the one will to save our Fatherland.
Our hurried steps are sounding on the long and arduous
road.

* Lac Long (Dragon Lord of the Lac) is regarded as the civilizing hero of the people from whom the Vietnamese descended. His reign—which belongs to Vietnamese mythology—was said to have been a golden age. Lac Long married a fairy named Au Co, who gave birth to a hundred boys, between whom the king and queen divided their kingdom. The eldest son was elected king under the name of Hong and became the founder of the first dynasty recognized by legend as genuinely Vietnamese.

Our flag, red with the blood of victory, bears the spirit of our country.
The distant rumbling of the guns mingles with our marching song.
The path to glory passes over the bodies of our foes.
Overcoming all hardships, together we build our resistance bases.
Ceaselessly for the people's cause we struggle.
Hastening to the battlefield!
Forward! All together advancing!
Our Vietnam is strong, eternal.

Verse 2

Soldiers of Vietnam, we go forward!
The gold star of our flag in the wind.
Leading our people, our native land, out of misery and suffering.
Let us join our efforts in the fight for the building of a new life.
Let us stand up and break our chains.
For too long have we swallowed our hatred.
Let us stay ready for all sacrifices and our life will be radiant.
Ceaselessly for the people's cause we struggle,
Hastening to the battlefield!
Forward! All together advancing!
Our Vietnam is strong, eternal.

POETS OF THE UNDERGROUND

"A POET WHO IS INVOLVED," BY *To Huu,* translated by *François Sully*

To Huu is a member of North Vietnam's ruling Lao Dong (Workers') Party and one of the intellectual luminaries of the Hanoi regime. Regarded as one of Vietnam's leading contemporary poets, To Huu was obviously influenced in his youth by such French poets of the nineteenth century as Rimbaud, Verlaine, and De Bainville.

Since

Since then, I, imbued with eternal summer
My heart lighted by the sun of truth *
My soul a garden in foliage and flower
Filled with scents and humming with life.

My heart I have attached to all living hearts
So that my love may be sown at large by the wind
My spirit I have bound to all suffering souls
That life in this communion may find its strength

Since then, I have been the child of thousands of homes
The younger son of thousands of humbled destinies

* Here, the poet probably evokes his admission to the Communist Lao Dong Party.

The older brother to thousands of children in tatters
Wandering with neither home nor hearth nor love nor
compassion.

The Dyed Green Jacket

Darling, would you dye my jacket green
A clear green, the color of the leaves
Because the war will not tolerate
The whiteness of a target or of our mourning * clothes.

Once again, I am in the rain and wind
My rifle on my shoulder, forward on
My jacket is green
As hope in the South: green with victory.

Under the bombs and shells
Through the days and nights of fighting
I will not think of danger
Because with this green of our villages.

My jacket dyed by your hands
Though it may be tattered and worn tomorrow
Will retain forever your warmth
And the freshness of our young love.

NIGHT CROSSING, BY *Giang Nam*

Giang Nam is regarded by militant intellectuals as one of the most promising young poets of the Vietnamese underground, or Viet Cong. Since he is using a pseudonym to sign his works, very little

* White, in Vietnam, is the traditional color of mourning.

is known about him, except that he often shares the dangers of his friends the partisans. In this war poem, Giang Nam tells the story of a small group of guerrillas crossing a river at night in a fragile sampan. Their guide is a young farm girl from the neighboring village. She is pretty and unafraid, even when government soldiers manning a guard-tower open fire on the boat. Crouching in the sampan, the guerrillas hold their fire, obviously afraid of the bullets raining around them. The cold-blooded young girl takes charge. Eventually, she will take the boat and its human cargo safely across the river. The guerrillas go on to their assigned mission, keeping in their memories the fond image of the brave boat-girl who saved their lives.

In the midst of the night, a sampan glides toward us.
Dark bamboos on the bank, swift current . . .
An oar shatters the star-studded firmament.
A bird wanders in the dark and disappears.
Silently the sampan glides between the palms
Whose crests are swept by a searchlight from the outpost.

Loaded rifles, all hands on alert,
We await the moment to dart across the river.

* * *

Tucking her black trousers up to her thigh
The boat-girl, smelling of grass and flowers, helps us
Unload our motley bundles.
In the dark, we imagine her red cheeks;
Holding her hand
We breathe her breath, sense her brisk gestures.

Loudly, the water clatters against the sampan.
Heavily loaded, it rolls and leaves the bank so slowly.
"Comrade" asks a voice, "can I help you?"
Shaking her head, she swings the bow.
In the midst of enemy outposts she lives
Keeping for herself the sorrow and joys of her heart.
The sampan emerges from the dark
Challenging the current, the onrushing wave,
Again the oar shatters the sky and the stars.
The other bank is silent, a palm greets us.
Standing still, our boat-girl is watching the guardpost
at the hamlet's entrance.
Her arms still swinging the oar.
Her slender silhouette looms over the river.
One more effort, and we will reach the bank;
A feeling of tender joy flushes our bodies.

A long burst has been fired from the outpost,
Red and white tracers thunder everywhere.
"Be quiet," she says, "don't be afraid,"
And the sampan swiftly
Darts toward the enemy, defying its bullets.
Silhouetted in the sky, what a dashing figure;
"Lie down," she whispers, "let me maneuver,
Don't be worried!" The boat moves ahead;
Emotion packs the night.
Our hearts are pinching; anger fills our eyes.
Bullets rain in the river.
In our hands, our rifles burn with anger.

In safe haven, the sampan is tied to a tree.
Slowly, we shake the girl's hand.
"Thank you," we say . . . A smile lights
her face; "I belong to the youth corps,
And I only do my duty," she answers.
We press our march across the village

Still thinking, still hearing
The light tread of her walk.

Valiant image, valiant girl
In future battles come with us.

I AM A FIGHTER OF THE LIBERATION ARMY, BY *Lien Nam*

The young poet, using the pseudonym of Lien Nam to protect his real identity, composes in free verse to express the emotions of an eighteen-year-old soldier of the Liberation Army, whose ideal is to "walk into the fight" and free his native land of the presence of foreign soldiers. Lien Nam's imagistic style conveys a series of clear, precise images familiar to any patriotic Vietnamese, in whatever camp he may serve.

I am a fighter
of the Liberation Army
crossing over valleys and mountains, rivers and torrents.
I am still young: eighteen years old
Full grown as the full moon
announcing many springs.
Sometimes without shirt or blanket
tortured by fever, I walk into the fight
without a bitter pill to ease my pain.
Sometimes under a burning sun
hatless and barefooted I walk
under the protection of the sky and heaven.
But facing the enemy who destroys everything,
even the green of the grass and of the trees,
I aim my rifle, for kill him I must
so, on my native land
tears may dry; more smiles may

bloom on children's lips,
so may ripen under the sun, the acorn of Dong Thap
so the salt of Sa Huynh may
lend its taste to our food in the mountains
O! so many dreams and hopes I carry with me,
burning sun of each of my days!
Even if my daily rice
is laced with manioc,
even if we have to clear the forests
to grow the red corn,
defying the mist and the storms,
the sun and the wind,
ready to endure a thousand tests
I march forward,
with unshakable will and strong heart
always present in the first ranks
of our great army!
I swear to remain
under the sacred flag of my motherland,
under the brilliant flag, dyed in
the fiery red of a heroic blood.
I swear to fight till my last breath
to erase from the land of the South
even the shadow of a foreign soldier
to bring bread, peace, liberty
over the entire sweep of my sacred motherland.
To give a worthy account of a fighter
of the Liberation Army of South Vietnam

I CROSSED THE DEMARCATION LINE, BY *Thanh Hai*

The poem tells the dream of a guerrilla's wife who remained in the South after the 1954 partition of Vietnam while her husband was regrouped in North Vietnam with the Viet Minh army. In dreams she crosses the Seventeenth Parallel and tells her husband that, despite pressures and beatings from the authorities, she refused to remarry as, apparently, some other women in her case did. Before their departure for North Vietnam, many of the Viet Minh guerrillas who had fought in the South took local wives, from whom they were separated after a honeymoon only a few days long.

Thanh Hai is a young poet who joined the National Liberation Front. His verses have been published in Vietnamese Studies, *Hanoi, 1967.*

Last night I crossed the demarcation line
On my way North to meet you.
For so long I had been thinking of you,
Oh, with what eager haste I walked.

I hurried along the rice fields
So beautifully green.
I went through the streets of the city,
Was it you, darling, I saw over there?

Oh yes, it was you—you—you
Yes it was you, darling. I broke into a run.
"Darling," I cried, "wait.
It's me, darling, wait for me."

You stopped. You had recognized
My figure from afar.
Even lost amidst a hundred thousand girls,
I would have caught your eyes right away.

And in your arms nestled,
I cried: "Five years have gone!"
You clasped me tight:
There were so many things to say!

You asked me about the fields,
The hamlet and the village.
Bitter, Oh bitter were those years,
How could I tell you all our sufferings.

You touched my round arm,
Where you used to rest your head.
With sudden anguish you asked,
"What's this scar in your flesh?

Who made that deep gash in your arm?"
"All these years I've waited for you,
I've not gone over to the enemy,
I've refused to take another husband.

Because I refused to forsake you,
The enemy hunted and arrested me.
It was they who made that deep cut
Where your head used to rest."

A cock crowed somewhere,
I awoke from my sleep,
The memory of my dream
Rent my heart with grief.

From the martyred South,
Oh, do you know it, dear?
Each night, to meet you, my heart
Crosses the demarcation line.

"FLOWERS OF TEARS," BY *Ha Huyen Chi*, translated by *Do Lenh Thuan*

This poem, which appeared in a South Vietnamese army magazine in 1966, is by a Vietna-

mese army captain, writing under the pseudonym of Ha Huyen Chi, who served in Quang Ngai Province with Captain Arnold Canarina, an adviser to the Vietnamese forces. Not one of the least strange aspects of the Vietnamese people is that a seasoned professional soldier could write poetry expressing his innermost feelings about a handsome blond American officer who has come to fight in his "wrinkled land where a bowl of rice is earned with a bowl of sweat." Translation into English is the work of Do Lenh Thuan, a Vietnamese diplomat in the United States.

Canarina,
The airborne soldier of America,
His hair the yellow of autumn leaves,
His eyes the blue of the rolling seas;
When grapes were ripe he left his native country.
To the land of the Viet he came,
To share with us the burden of war.
He told me of his country
Land of golden shores and maple leaves,
Factories and buildings reaching the clouds of heaven.
Land of seven Sundays,
Nights of million stars, days of song and laughter.
I offered him the first taste of hardship,
An endless war
In a miserable country.
Nights of sleep among swampy reeds, lying in ambush,
Days of crossing rivers and climbing mountains, pursuing
the enemy.
Muddy water for drink, bitter fruits for meals.
There you see
My country, land of wrinkles, mountains of rocks,
Empty gardens, crumbling huts—desolation.

Undernourished people, faces as green as banana leaves,
Children, round bellies and flat chests,
Greet you with soulless eyes—desperation.
You see my people,
Their lives a perpetual hardship;
A bowl of sweat for a bowl of rice.
There are forests to clear, mountains to level,
Fields to irrigate without rain,
Land to plough without buffalo,
Bony shoulders covered with thin clothes;
But long days of hard work seem nothing.

Canarina,
The airborne soldier of America,
His hair the yellow of autumn leaves,
His eyes the blue of the rolling seas.
One year of combat,
More than once wounded,
He mixed his blood with ours
Strengthening the bonds of friendship forever.
He learned to live and eat like a Viet;
Together, we washed with the rain and bathed with the wind,
Together, we had earth for bed and clouds for blanket.
Fearless of obstacles, unappalled by hardship,
His blond hair blonder from the sun and fire,
His blue eyes bluer from the pain of life,
How sad the day for his return home,
Silence and tears in his eyes;
Tears also from my men,
The flowers of tears born out of friendship.
He mumbled a few Vietnamese words,
"I love Vietnam and shall remember you."

FOLK SONGS OF PROTEST

"I HAD A LOVER" and "MOTHER'S HERITAGE," BY *Trinh Cong Son*, translated by *François Sully*

Perhaps the best illustration of South Vietnam's war-weariness is the music of Trinh Cong Son, a thirty-year-old folk singer born in Hue, in central Vietnam. Son's poignant lyrics convey the profound melancholy of the Vietnamese people, their frustrations and their wishful dreams of peace. Although Son's music has been banned from the government-controlled radio and television stations, he is still the most popular folk singer in the country.

I Had a Lover

I had a lover. He died on the battlefield of Pleime
I had a lover. He died on the battlefield of Dong Xoai
I had a lover. He died in Hanoi. He died in War Zone D.
He died on the frontier.
I had a lover. He died on the battlefield of Chu Prong.
I had a lover. His body lies in a river, in a rice field, in the woods.
He died. His body became cold and was burned to ashes.

I want to love you. Love Vietnam.
The day when the wind is strong, I wander

With my lips whispering your name, the name of
Vietnam
And we are so close, of the same voice and yellow race
I want to love you. Love Vietnam.
I have just grown up and my ears are already familiar
with the sound of bullets.

Useless are my arms,
Useless are my lips,
From now on, I shall forget your voice.

I had a lover. He died on the battlefield of A Shau.
I had a lover. He died in some valley. His body broken.
He died under a bridge, naked and voiceless.
I had a lover. He died on the battlefield of Ba Gia.*
I had a lover. He died only yesterday, suddenly, without
hate.
He died as a dreamer.

Mother's Heritage

A thousand years dominated by the Chinese
A hundred years enslaved by the French.
Then twenty years of destructive fratricidal war,
day after day.
Mother! What heritage have you left to your children?
Mother! Your heritage is Vietnam in sorrow.

A thousand years dominated by the Chinese
A hundred years enslaved by the French.
Then twenty years of destructive fratricidal war,
day after day.
Mother! Your heritage is a forest of dry bones.
Mother! Your heritage is an immense graveyard.

* Pleime, Dong Xoai, Chu Prong, A Shau, and Ba Gia are the names of battles costly in human lives. War Zone D is a well-known guerrilla base northeast of Saigon.

Children! Learn from me the voice of truth.
I hope you will never forget the color of your skin.
The color of Vietnam of old.
I hope you will be home soon.
Oh children faraway! Oh children of the same father!
I am looking forward to seeing you; forget your hates.

A thousand years dominated by the Chinese
A hundred years enslaved by the French.
Then twenty years of destructive fratricidal war,
  day after day.
Mother! Your heritage is parched rice fields.
Mother! Your heritage is rows of homes in flames.

A thousand years dominated by the Chinese
A hundred years enslaved by the French.
Then twenty years of destructive fratricidal war,
  day after day.
Mother! Your heritage is a horde of rootless people.
Mother! Your heritage is a horde of traitors.

"DON'T PICK THE FLOWER WHEN IT IS BLOOMING" and "THE MOTHER OF 'GIO LINH,' " BY *Pham Duy*

Pham Duy was born in North Vietnam about thirty-five years ago. Singing his patriotic songs in the style of a modern troubador, he took part in the anti-French resistance as a member of a Viet Minh song-and-dance troupe. But in 1954, when the war was over, Pham Duy left his native home to come South. Pham Duy's songs reflect the past, but they also reflect present days, love, work, and the long and bitter years of war. Pham Duy has collected old folk songs of North Vietnam to make modern lyrics that have become popular among Vietnamese students and musicians.

Don't Pick the Flower When It Is Blooming

My friend, you must pick the flowers with skill;
Cut only those that have faded,
Don't let them die on the stalk.

The wind blows from afar and the flowers are blooming;
Loving their scent, I don't like to pick them;
When the wind blows, the flowers smile.

The butterfly plays with the flowers, and kisses them;
The flower that shows its affection will be old the soonest;
The butterfly plays, and the flower suffers.

The children play with the flowers, they pick them with no regrets;
The innocent flowers are looking for love;
Don't let the fairy garden become empty.

The Mother of "Gio Linh" *

The old mother digs the ground to plant potatoes
To nourish her son who is fighting the enemy day and night.
Even her dress is ragged and there is not enough to eat.
The enemy has burned our house, and we plan to revenge ourselves;
The mother is glad that her son is a good fighter.
She works very, very hard. Her son enjoys going to battle.

* Gio Linh is a small, hilly village of Quang Tri Province, just south of the Seventeenth Parallel, the temporary partition line between North and South Vietnam.

The old mother has only one son, but her love of her country is not inferior to anyone's.
At night, hearing the sound of battle, she prays for her son.

The old mother was watering the vegetables when she heard the cry of the villagers;
The enemy has caught her son, and now they conduct him to the market, and they cut off his head.
The mother is speechless; she goes forward to get the head of her son.
On the road to the village there is a pagoda and now its bell sounds once heavily.
The mother takes in her hands the head of her son, her eyes are full of tears.
She looks at him, her white hair flowing in the breeze.
"Ah, I love my son. Though his mouth is bloody there is a smile on his face and his eyes look at me."

The old mother prepares the tea every night, looking for someone . . . .
The guns thud in the distance, and orphans and widows are sad.
Everyday I come to visit the old mother, to sit by the hearth;
She cooks a pot of potatoes and the smoke is like incense.
She misses her son, but now she has many adopted sons to look after . . . .
"O my sons, finish your cup of tea and come often to visit me!"

SUGGESTIONS FOR FURTHER READING

Buttinger, Joseph. The Smaller Dragon: A Political History of Vietnam. New York: Praeger, 1958.

Chung, Ly Qui, Editor. Between Two Fires: The Unheard Voices of Vietnam. New York: Praeger, 1970.

Fall, Bernard B. Street Without Joy, rev. ed. Harrisburg, Pa.: Stackpole, 1966.

Fall, Bernard B. The Two Viet-Nams: A Political and Military Analysis, 2nd rev. ed. New York: Praeger, 1967.

Halberstam, David. The Making of a Quagmire. New York: Random House, 1965.

Schultz, George F. Vietnamese Legends and Other Tales. Rutland, Vermont: C. E. Tuttle, 1965.

INDEX